GRADE

Grammar and Writing Handbook

ISBN: 0–328–07540–X

3 4 5 6 7 8 9 10 V000 09 08 07 06 05 04

scottforesman.com

Editorial Offices: Glenview, Illinois • Parsippany, New Jersey • New York, New York
Sales Offices: Parsippany, New Jersey • Duluth, Georgia • Glenview, Illinois
Coppell, Texas • Ontario, California • Mesa, Arizona

TABLE OF CONTENTS

Writer's Guide   5

Ideas and Content   6
Organization   8
Voice   10
Word Choice   12
Sentences   14
Conventions   16
Using a Scoring Rubric   18
Writing Models   19

Grammar and Writing Lessons   23

Unit 1   **Grammar** Sentences   24
Writing Telling About *You* in Personal Narratives   27
Grammar Subjects and Predicates   28
Writing Adding Details to Subjects and Predicates   31
Grammar Declarative and Interrogative Sentences   32
Writing Varying Sentence Style   35
Grammar Imperative and Exclamatory Sentences   36
Writing Making Your Narrative Exciting   39
Grammar Compound and Complex Sentences   40
Writing Combining Sentences   43
Writing for Tests Personal Narrative   44

Unit 2   **Grammar** Nouns   46
Writing Using Exact Common Nouns in Descriptions   49
Grammar Proper Nouns   50
Writing Using Proper Nouns in Descriptions   53
Grammar Regular Plural Nouns   54

Writing Using Plural Nouns in Descriptions   **57**

Grammar Irregular Plural Nouns   **58**

Writing Using Irregular Plural Nouns in Descriptions   **61**

Grammar Possessive Nouns   **62**

Writing Using Possessive Nouns in Descriptions   **65**

Writing for Tests Description   **66**

Unit 3

Grammar Verbs   **68**

Writing Replacing Forms of *Be* with Action Verbs   **71**

Grammar Verbs in Sentences   **72**

Writing Using Verbs in Comparisons   **75**

Grammar Verb Tenses: Present, Past, and Future   **76**

Writing Using Correct Verb Tenses in Your Writing   **79**

Grammar Using Correct Verb Tenses   **80**

Writing Replacing Dull Verbs   **83**

Grammar Review of Verbs   **84**

Writing Using Powerful Verbs in Your Writing   **87**

Writing for Tests Comparison/Contrast Essay   **88**

Unit 4

Grammar Adjectives   **90**

Writing Using Clear Adjectives in Your Writing   **93**

Grammar Using Adjectives to Improve Sentences   **94**

Writing Using Adjectives to Improve Sentences   **97**

Grammar Comparative and Superlative Adjectives   **98**

Writing Making Comparisons in Your Writing   **101**

Grammar Adverbs   **102**

Writing Using Adverbs to Show Time Order   **105**

Grammar Using Adverbs to Improve Sentences   **106**

Writing Using Adverbs to Improve Sentences   **109**

Writing for Tests How-to Report   **110**

Unit 5

Grammar Pronouns   **112**

Writing Using Pronouns to Improve Your Style   **115**

Grammar Subject and Object Pronouns   **116**

Writing Using Subject and Object Pronouns   **119**

Grammar Pronouns and Referents   **120**

Writing Using Pronouns in Your Writing   **123**

Grammar Prepositions and Prepositional Phrases   **124**

Writing Using Prepositional Phrases to Add Details   **127**

Grammar Conjunctions   **128**

Writing Using Conjunctions to Improve Your Style   **131**

Writing for Tests Summary   **132**

Unit 6

Grammar Sentences and Punctuation   **134**

Writing Varying Sentences in Your Writing   **137**

Grammar Capitalization   **138**

Writing Observing the Rules for Capitalization   **141**

Grammar Commas   **142**

Writing Making Writing Clear with Commas   **145**

Grammar Quotations and Quotation Marks   **146**

Writing Using Quotations to Support Your Opinions   **149**

Grammar Review of Compound and Complex Sentences   **150**

Writing Varying Sentences to Strengthen Your Style   **153**

Writing for Tests Persuasive Argument   **154**

Index   **156**

Writer's Guide

Ideas and Content

Good writers set out with a **main idea** and a **purpose** in mind. The main idea is the point they want to make. The purpose is how they will make that point. Will the writing inform, persuade, or entertain readers?

Even a phone message has a main idea and a purpose.

Mom,
   Sam has a ride home
   from soccer tonight
   with Mr. Kim. He will be
   here by 6.
                  Jamie

Main Idea How and when Sam will get home
Purpose To inform Mom

FOCUS

Everything you write should support your main idea. Details that are off the subject or unimportant weaken writing.

Details Details support and develop your main idea. This telephone note tells Mom who is driving Sam and when he is arriving. These details give important information. Details can also make writing lively and interesting. Compare the two sentences below.

Our dog likes candy. (lacks detail)
Our collie Shadow cocks her head and wags her tail
   when she hears a candy wrapper crinkle. (adds interest)

Strategies for Choosing a Topic and a Purpose

- Choose a topic that you can work with. For example, "Famous Presidents" is too large a topic for a one-paragraph essay.
- Choose a purpose that fits your topic. For example, a funny story would entertain readers, but an article on war might not.

A Match the number of each writing assignment with the letter of the purpose that best suits it.

> **A** To entertain   **B** To inform   **C** To persuade

1. Arguments for year-round school
2. A recipe
3. A story about a funny day at school

B Read the paragraph below. Write the number of any sentence that does not focus on the main idea stated in the first sentence.

4. The colors of wildflowers attract animals for pollination. 5. Yellow lantana flowers attract butterflies. 6. Blue flowers are my favorite. 7. Birds like bright red poppies. 8. Wind also helps pollinate flowers. 9. The colorful birthwort flower attracts flies, covers them with pollen, and then lets them escape. 10. One flower even smells like rotten meat to attract flies.

C Complete one of the following sentences to begin a paragraph. Then write three sentences of your own to give details about the first sentence.

_____ make the best pets.
The best movie I ever saw was _____.
My favorite season is _____.
_____ is the best sport.

Organization

When you write, you need to put ideas in an order that makes sense. **Organization**—the way ideas are put together—is like the skeleton of a body. It holds things together and gives shape.

Here are some ways to organize your writing.

- a story with a beginning, middle, and end
- a comparison-contrast
- a step-by-step explanation
- a description from top to bottom

Before you begin to write, think of the best way to put your ideas together. For example, if you are describing how two best friends are alike and different, a comparison-contrast would work. If you are telling about something that happened to you, a story form would be good.

Choosing a basic structure is only the first step in organizing your writing. You will also need to connect your ideas and make them move from beginning to end.

Strategies for Organizing Ideas

- Save the most important idea until last and build up to it.
- Use sequence words such as *first, next, tomorrow,* and *finally.*
- Use connectors such as *but* and *however* to show differences and *too* and *also* to show likenesses.

GRAPHIC ORGANIZER

A graphic organizer such as a web, Venn diagram, or outline can help you organize your ideas.

A Match the number of each writing assignment below with the letter of the organization it calls for.

    A Description   **C** Comparison-contrast
    B Story   **D** Step-by-step explanation

1. Tell about what happened on your first day of school.
2. Explain how to find information on the Internet.
3. Tell how baseball is different from soccer.
4. Describe a friend from head to toe.

B Write the best word or words from the Connecting Words box to make each sentence flow smoothly.

Connecting Words		
However	Finally	For example
First	Next	

    Pets are fun. **5.** _____, they are also work. **6.** _____ of all, before getting a pet, consider how much care it will need. Remember that a dog needs to be walked, but a hamster does not. **7.** _____, think about what kind of pet suits your home. **8.** _____, if you live in an apartment, a small animal may be a better pet than a large one. **9.** _____, ask yourself where your pet will live. Are you willing to share your room if you have to?

C Think of a machine, toy, tool, or similar object. Write a step-by-step explanation that tells how this object works. Use words such as *first, next, now,* and *finally* to show the steps in order.

Voice

Voice is the *you* that comes through in your writing and makes it interesting. Voice reveals tone and style, as well as your personality. Writers with a strong voice engage their readers and speak directly to them. Voice shows that the writer knows a topic and cares about it.

- When I was young, I didn't like asparagus. (weak voice)
- I used to cry in my highchair, as I pushed slimy green asparagus off my plate. It looked like snakes. (strong voice)

Strategies for Developing Your Voice

- Know your purpose and audience. A story about a funny event written to a friend should have a light, playful voice. A research paper for your teacher should have a serious, well-informed voice.
- Choose words to match your voice. Persuasive writing requires words such as *should, best,* and *most important.* Informal language, perhaps exaggeration or even slang, suits a friendly, casual voice. Figurative language can add a strong voice. A business letter requires objective, precise word choice.
- Remember that all good writing needs a voice to hold a reader's interest. Voice should be engaging, lively, and interesting. Let your readers know how you feel about your subject.

> **VOICE**
>
> **Voice makes writing come to life. Depending on the topic, voice may be lively, honest, excited, humorous, or suspenseful.**

A Match the numbered item with the type of writing it is.

    A Newspaper article   **C** Business letter
    B Humorous article   **D** Persuasive piece

1. Please send me a year's subscription to *Campers' Guide.*
   Enclosed is a check for $15.
2. Our class must help save our universe by recycling.
3. After Sanpa ate corn, buttered kernels glowed on his beard
   like jewels. I expect to see birds nesting there one day.
4. At noon today a crowd of 2,000 cheered the *Cambridge*
   lift-off from Cape Kennedy.

B Each underlined part of the following business letter has a "voice problem." Match the letter of the problem with each numbered item.

    A Unnecessary information   **C** Slang
    B Inappropriate humor   **D** Overly formal language

Dear Channel 29:
    5. Your TV special on sunken treasures was <u>way cool</u>. **6.** I have <u>perused publications</u> about this topic. **7.** Where did you ever <u>"dig up" (ha!)</u> all those photographs? **8.** Could you please send me more information <u>so I can raise my grade, which I desperately need to do</u>?
Kyra Sathers

C Complete one of the following statements. Then add sentences to write a paragraph. Use a voice that fits your topic.

I like (do not like) people who _____ because _____.
If I could be an animal, I would be a _____ because _____.
My favorite memory is _____ because _____.

Word Choice

Have you noticed that good writers choose their **words** carefully? Strong verbs, exact nouns, and vivid adjectives make their writing clear and lively.

- Kids don't like that dog because of the fact that he's mean. (dull and wordy)
- Kids scream when Rusty snarls and lunges on his leash. (lively)

Strategies for Improving Word Choice

- Use specific nouns. (*canary* instead of *bird*, *ballerina* instead of *dancer*)
- Use strong verbs. (*wriggle* instead of *move*, *splinter* instead of *break*)
- Appeal to the senses. ("My teeth are chattering" instead of "I am cold," "hair looks like spun gold" instead of "hair looks pretty")
- Consider rewriting sentences that have *is*, *was*, *were*, *am*, and *are*. ("My stomach churned" instead of "I was sick")
- Replace words such as *nice*, *great*, *thing*, and *stuff* with exact words. ("I collect coins and stamps" instead of "I collect things")
- Get rid of wordiness. (*because* instead of "due to the fact that")

"Wow" Words

Be on the lookout for "wow" words that make writing come alive: *silky, shiver, syrup, ker-plunk, slurp, dazzle, slimy, splatter.* Keep a notebook handy to record these words.

A Choose the word that is more vivid or exact to complete each sentence. Write the sentence.

1. The baby (called, whimpered) for her mother.
2. The car (clattered, moved) down the road.
3. (Old, Wilted) flowers lined the sidewalk.
4. Max (spoke, muttered) his speech in the play.
5. I (stumbled, went) down the path.
6. The angry bulls (ran, stampeded).
7. Water (went, sprayed) all over the kitchen.

B Replace an underlined word with a word or words from the box. Rewrite each sentence.

snatch	helium balloon	stilt-like
nibble	giraffes	bulge

8. Sometimes we watch <u>animals</u> at the zoo. 9. They walk on <u>weird</u> legs. 10. Their eyes <u>look</u> out. 11. It's fun to see them <u>eat</u> leaves from the high branches of trees. 12. One time I saw a giraffe <u>take</u> something. 13. It was a little boy's <u>toy</u>.

C Write a description of your favorite place outdoors. Use vivid words that appeal to the senses.

Sentences

Good writing flows smoothly. It is a pleasure to read aloud. Different lengths and kinds of **sentences** create a rhythm and style.

Here are some ways to improve your sentences.

- Vary sentence length. Avoid having all short, simple sentences.
- Vary sentence types. An interrogative, imperative, or exclamatory sentence can add excitement.
- Use different beginnings. Too many sentences beginning with *I, he,* or *the* make for a dull style.
- Use connectors. Words such as *first, but, and, although, while,* and *however* make sentences flow smoothly. However, do not connect too many ideas with *so, and,* or *because.*

Strategy for Improving Sentences

Number each sentence of your writing. Then make a chart like this.

Sentence number	Number of words	First word	Type of sentence (Interrogative, Declarative, Imperative, Exclamatory)	Connector words

Filling out your chart may reveal areas to improve. You may learn that you write mostly short declarative sentences beginning with *the* or *I.* You may learn that you use the word *and* to string too many ideas together. When you revise your work, try to improve these areas.

A Combine these short, choppy sentences. Use the connector provided. Write the sentences.

> **Example:** The plants froze. No one brought them in. *(because)*
> **Answer:** The plants froze because no one brought them in.

1. Ted made the hockey team. He's only ten. *(although)*
2. Luis stayed home. He had a cold. *(because)*
3. Mother painted. I played my violin. *(while)*
4. We tried. We lost. *(but)*

B In the paragraph below, rearrange words in each sentence so that it does not begin with *I*. Start with the underlined word or phrase. Write the sentences.

> **Example:** I got Tinker <u>last fall</u> from my dad.
> **Answer:** Last fall I got Tinker from my dad.

5. I had begged for a tropical fish <u>for years</u>. 6. I went with my dad <u>one Saturday</u> to Pet Scope. 7. I saw the striped fish that I wanted <u>immediately</u>. 8. I named him Tinker <u>in the car</u>. 9. I filled the fish tank with water <u>before lunch</u>. 10. I get to buy two more fish <u>next year</u>.

C Write a description of your favorite food, friend, book, TV program, or sport. Include one interrogative and one exclamatory sentence. Make sure each sentence begins with a different word.

Writing Sentences

Conventions

Conventions are the rules for written language. They are signals that help readers understand writing. For example, sentences begin with capital letters and end with punctuation. Paragraphs are indented. Grammar and spelling follow patterns.

- me and willie ax mama aunt belle and max the question we didnt get a answr. (weak conventions)
- Willie and I asked Mama, Aunt Belle, and Max the question. We didn't get an answer. (strong conventions)

Strategies for Conventions

- Use a dictionary or spell-checker to check spelling.
- Make sure sentences are complete, with correct capitalization and punctuation.
- Check that subjects and verbs agree.
- Make sure you have used the correct forms of pronouns, especially pronouns that are compound subjects or objects.
- Make sure you haven't changed verb tenses by mistake.
- Check the use of apostrophes in possessive nouns and contractions.

PROOFREADING MARKS	
¶	New paragraph
≡	Capital letter
/	Lowercase letter
◯	Correct the spelling.
∧	Add something.
ℒ	Remove something.

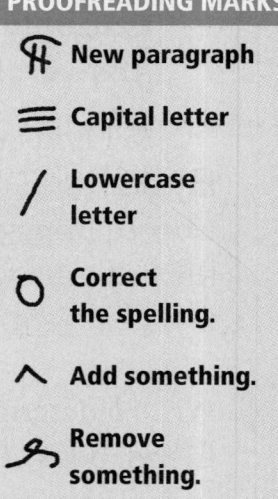

A Choose the correct answer and write each sentence.

1. (There, They're) planning to go to California.
2. Sally and (me, I) will meet in San Francisco.
3. Sam has (went, gone) there already.
4. I (was'nt, wasn't) going to take the train.
5. Give (her and me, she and I) the test.

PROOFREADING

A good proofreader is a detective. Look closely for mistakes. Here are some tricks to catch errors. Start reading in the middle of your work. Use a ruler to go line by line. Read your work aloud.

B Match the letter with the mistake in each sentence.

A Capitalize a proper noun.
B End sentence with a question mark.
C Correct a misspelling.
D Add an apostrophe.
E Change a capital letter to lowercase.

6. Humpback whales are talented singers of the Sea.
7. These creatures odd sounds range from chirps and moans to bellows and belches. 8. Underwater, there songs can be heard for miles. 9. Did you know that a humpback can eat a ton of food a day. 10. Each year, people go to Australia and hawaii to see these interesting creatures.

C Write four sentences about one of the topics below. Pay special attention to spelling, grammar, punctuation, and capitalization. Exchange papers with a partner and proofread.

- Something I would like to change
- Someone I would like to meet
- Somewhere I would like to go

Using a Scoring Rubric

What makes an *excellent* piece of writing? How is it different from writing that is *good*, or *not good?* One way to judge a written work is to use a scoring **rubric.** A rubric is a checklist of *qualities*, or things to look for. See pages 6–17 for a discussion of these qualities.

Rubrics give a number score for each quality. You can use a rubric such as the one below to judge your writing.

SCORE	IDEAS/CONTENT	ORGANIZATION	VOICE	WORD CHOICE	SENTENCES	CONVENTIONS
4	Clear, focused, well-supported ideas	Smooth flow of ideas from beginning to end, with connecting words	Honest, engaging, lively writing	Precise, interesting, and accurate words	Smooth, varied, and rhythmic sentences	Excellent control with only minor errors
3	Ideas usually focused and supported	Information given in some order	At times reveals writer's personality	Correct and adequate words	Generally smooth, varied sentences	Good control; no serious errors prevent understanding
2	Ideas sometimes unfocused and undeveloped	Little direction from beginning to end	Fails to engage audience or show emotion	Limited vocabulary; lacks freshness	Awkward or wordy sentences with little variety	Weak control with errors that make writing hard to read
1	Ideas confusing and unsupported	Ideas hard to follow with no direction	Flat writing with no feeling	Incorrect, dull, or overused words	Choppy sentences; run-ons or fragments; *and* overused as connector	Many errors that prevent understanding

Writing Models

Following are four responses to a prompt. Read the responses and the notes below them to see how each piece got its score.

Writing Prompt: Write about an accident you had and how someone helped.

> I was running from the pool after swimming practice when I skidded on the slippery cement. Splat! I could taste blood and started to shiver. My mom grabbed me and soon we were in the emergancy room. Instead of stiches they used special glue on my lip. It stung and smelled nasty. While we waited for the glue to dry. Mom read me a book about alligators in the Everglades. Finally I was in one piece again! Next time, I won't run.

SCORE 4
Ideas/Content Focused on the accident; supported with details
Organization Connectors *soon, while,* and *finally* move story along; has a clear ending
Voice Strongly engages readers (*Splat!, nasty*)
Word Choice Vivid word choice and images (*skidded, slippery,* "taste blood")
Sentences Varied, clear sentences with good rhythms
Conventions Some misspellings (*stiches, emergancy*)

It was my first day at Bell School. I slipped on some butter in the cafeteria. Macroni and peas sprayed all over due to the fact that I dropped my tray. My shirt was soaked with milk. I was so embarased. I wanted to crawl under a table. Bill Mellis gave me his napkin to wipe things up. He went back in the line with me to get another lunch. He's like my best friend now. We both laugh when they serve mac and cheese and peas on Mondays.

SCORE 3

Ideas/Content Focused on the accident and supported with many details

Organization Could add connectors such as *then* to make events flow more smoothly; has a clear ending

Voice Writer's feelings revealed ("I wanted to crawl...")

Word Choice Good use of verbs *(sprayed, crawl)*

Sentences Some wordiness ("due to the fact that," "like"); could combine some short sentences

Conventions A few mistakes; some spelling errors *(Macroni, embarased)*

When I was stuck because I got my tugh on a frosen stick and my mom came and calls the police. They put hot water on me and it was so hot it burned my tugh. I learned my lesson. Then my little sister was going to put her tugh on a stick and I whet runing and tell her don't do it because they will put hot water on you. She says she won't do that any more.

SCORE 2

Ideas/Content Focused on the accident but needs more supporting details

Organization Moves from a beginning to an end

Voice Gives readers a sense of who the writer is

Word Choice Limited, dull word choice (*got, put*)

Sentences Opens with a fragment; wordy

Conventions Misspellings (*tugh, frosen, whet, runing*), shifts in verb tense ("my mom came and calls")

> My mom helpt me But it did not work She send me to the haspetal and I Stay on the First Day I ate sooup and on the Secont Day I ate more Sooup and on the last Day I ate pizza and I leave

SCORE 1

Ideas/Content No explanation of what the accident was; lacks meaningful content and development

Organization Ideas arranged into three days

Voice Writer not involved

Word Choice Limited, dull word choice

Sentences No clear sentences or end punctuation; overuse of the connector *and*

Conventions Incorrect capitalization, misspellings *(helpt, haspetal, sooup, Secont)*, and tense shifts *(send, Stay, leave)*

Grammar and Writing Lessons

Sentences

A **sentence** is a group of words that expresses a complete thought. Sentences are used to tell, ask, command, or exclaim. All sentences begin with a capital letter and end with a punctuation mark.

Sentence: I will visit my grandfather.
Not a sentence: Will visit my grandfather.

A Read each group of words. Write **S** if it is a sentence. Write **NS** if it is not a sentence.

1. Made breakfast in the morning.
2. I hate making my bed!
3. We always sweep the porch at night.
4. Could you help do some chores?
5. Why the dishes?

Choose the word or group of words in ( ) that will complete each sentence. Write the complete sentence.

6. _____ works on a ranch. (Grandpa/Rides)
7. He _____. (a house/lives in a house)
8. _____ fed all the animals on his ranch. (We/Look)
9. Grandpa _____. (and I/gets up early)
10. _____ does his chores every day. (He/Cleans)
11. He _____. (washes the dishes/quietly)
12. _____ are going to a festival. (Every day/He and I)

B Write the group of words in each pair that is a sentence.

1. The cowboy rode a horse.
   Many famous cowboys.
2. Rodeos are fun.
   Places to see cowboys.
3. Bust broncos and drive cattle.
   Cowboys work hard.
4. Cowboys sing songs.
   Sit around the campfire.
5. Cowboys on a ranch?
   Do you want to be a cowboy?
6. Bill Pickett was a famous cowboy.
   Met a famous cowboy.
7. On the prairie.
   Wild horses run free.
8. Look at the cowboy!
   At the cowgirl?

C Add a word or group of words to complete each sentence.
Write the complete sentences.

9. Every morning I _____.
10. _____ can't find my shoes.
11. _____ eat a big breakfast.
12. Then I _____.
13. Before lunch I _____.
14. _____ run and play in the meadow.

Review and Assess

Read each group of words. Write **S** if it is a sentence. Write **NS** if it is not a sentence.

1. Many animals live on a ranch.
2. Are cows, horses, and birds?
3. Cardinals like to sing and whistle.
4. Cattle eat hay, grass, and corn.
5. Sometimes leap the fence.

Read each group of words. Write the letter of the word or group of words that will make a complete sentence.

6. Three young deer _____ through the forest.

    A baby   **C** slowly
    B girl   **D** ran

7. _____ likes to be bitten by mosquitoes.

    A Nobody   **C** Enjoys
    B Rarely   **D** Hurt

8. Wild horses _____ during the night.

    A always   **C** the road
    B noisy   **D** escaped

9. The rabbit _____ through the grass.

    A bunny   **C** hopped
    B fur   **D** under

10. The old dog _____ on the porch.

    A or cat   **C** yesterday
    B under   **D** slept

Telling About *You* in Personal Narratives

Personal narratives tell about an interesting event or experience in your life. They should include sentences about how you feel and look and what you do. Be sure to use complete sentences.

A Complete the sentences below with details from the box. Write the new paragraph.

Feel	looks forward to my visits; really enjoy
Look	in an old straw hat; shorts and a T-shirt
Act	weed; swimming in the pool; take photos

1. I _____ spending July with my grandpa in Maine. **2.** I can tell that Gramps _____. **3.** Every morning he is out in his garden _____. **4.** I put on _____ and join him. **5.** We _____ in the garden all morning. **6.** After gardening I cool off by _____ at the park. **7.** Then I walk around and _____ for a scrapbook of these special visits.

B Tell about yourself by completing these sentences. Write the sentences.

8. My favorite thing to wear is _____.
9. I am happy when I _____.
10. I will never forget _____.
11. When I was small, I _____.
12. When I'm excited, I _____.

WHO ARE YOU?

Tell about *you* in your narrative— your smile, the way you dress, or your favorite things to do.

C Write a personal narrative about a place or person that you have visited. Tell how you felt, looked, and acted.

Subjects and Predicates

The **subject** is the word or group of words that tells whom or what the sentence is about. The **simple subject** is the main noun or pronoun in the **complete subject**. The **predicate** is the word or group of words that tells something about the subject. The **simple predicate** is the verb in the **complete predicate**. A simple subject and a simple predicate can be more than one word.

Complete Subject	Complete Predicate	Simple Subject	Simple Predicate

The train arrived in the station.   The train arrived in the station.

A Write each sentence. Underline the complete subject and circle the complete predicate.

1. The train was fast.
2. Ken read a book on the train.
3. Many trains leave in the morning.
4. The train conductor smiled.
5. He checked my ticket and winked at me.

Write each sentence. Underline the simple subject once and the simple predicate twice.

6. I love trains.
7. Some trains are very long.
8. I have seen some small trains too.
9. Mrs. Grant will take me on the train next week.
10. We are planning a trip to the museum.

B Identify the underlined word or words in each sentence. Write **CS** for complete subjects, **CP** for complete predicates, **SS** for simple subjects, or **SP** for simple predicates.

1. My sister Pam <u>is a good traveling partner</u>.
2. We often <u>travel</u> together.
3. One day <u>Pam</u> and I took a train trip.
4. <u>The trip to Utah</u> took three days.
5. She <u>was sleeping on the seat next to me</u>.
6. We <u>were</u> nervous so far away from home.
7. Most of the time, though, <u>we</u> both enjoyed the trip.
8. We both <u>are looking</u> forward to the return trip.

C Finish each sentence by adding a complete subject or a complete predicate from the box below.

Complete Subject	Complete Predicate
Some people	prefer traveling by plane today
Planes and trains	took trains to travel long distances

9. People living one hundred years ago _____. 10. _____ still like to travel by train. 11. Many people _____. 12. _____ are both fun to ride.

Review and Assess

Read this paragraph. Then write the complete subjects in one column and the complete predicates in a second column.

1. My mother has lived in many places. **2.** She was born in Bristol, Connecticut. **3.** She and her family moved to Cleveland, Ohio, in 1975. **4.** My mother went to college in Iowa. **5.** Mom, Dad, my sisters, and I live in Georgia now.

Read each sentence. Write the letter of the words that describe the underlined words in each sentence.

6. <u>Juan Díaz</u>, our friend, was born in Chicago.

    A complete subject   **C** complete predicate
    B simple subject   **D** simple predicate

7. <u>Juan and his family</u> moved to Detroit two years ago.

    A complete subject   **C** complete predicate
    B simple subject   **D** simple predicate

8. He <u>has lived</u> there ever since.

    A complete subject   **C** complete predicate
    B simple subject   **D** simple predicate

9. Juan <u>likes living there</u>.

    A complete subject   **C** complete predicate
    B simple subject   **D** simple predicate

10. He <u>has</u> many friends.

    A complete subject   **C** complete predicate
    B simple subject   **D** simple predicate

Adding Details to Subjects and Predicates

Add details to make your personal narrative come alive. Tell what you saw, how you felt, and what happened.

SPECIFIC DETAILS

Specific details can help readers enjoy your personal narrative.

- The train pulled into the station. The doors opened.
- The train, huffing and puffing, pulled into the station. The heavy doors opened with a big clang.

A Complete the sentences below with details from the box.

> **Saw** bright red dress; giant puffy clouds
> **Felt** was excited; were both happy
> **What Happened** flew to Seattle; played tick-tack-toe

1. Last Friday Mom and I _____ to visit my cousin. **2.** From the window of the plane, we saw _____. **3.** I _____ to find out that the girl in front of us was my age. **4.** She was wearing a _____ and seemed friendly. **5.** We talked and _____ until we landed. **6.** After we exchanged e-mail addresses, we said that we _____ to make friends.

B Add details to these sentences to make this personal narrative come alive. Then write the new personal narrative.

7. I like to go to _____ (Name a place.) because _____ .
8. This place makes me feel _____. (Tell your feelings about this place.)
9. I could take photos of _____ . (Tell what you see there.)

C Write a narrative about a trip you took. Be sure to include details that tell what happened, what you saw and did, and how you felt.

Declarative and Interrogative Sentences

A **declarative sentence**, or statement, is a sentence that tells something. Declarative sentences end with a period. An **interrogative sentence**, or question, is a sentence that asks something. Interrogative sentences end with a question mark. Sentences begin with a capital letter.

Declarative sentence: I like all kinds of music.
Interrogative sentence: Do you like all kinds of music?

A Write **D** if the sentence is declarative.
Write **I** if the sentence is interrogative.

1. I really like to play guitar.
2. When I am tired, I like to listen to music.
3. When do you like to listen to music?
4. In the morning, I listen to station WBDX.
5. Do you like to listen to the radio?

Write each sentence with the correct end punctuation mark.

6. Do I have to listen to that song again
7. It sounds like two cats having a fight
8. This is not a song I would like to sing
9. Did this composer write any other songs
10. Maybe I would like those songs more than this one

B Write each sentence and add the correct end punctuation.
Then write whether each sentence is *declarative* or *interrogative*.

1. Where were you born
2. I was born in China
3. When I was younger, I lived in Virginia
4. Now I live in Washington
5. Do you like your town
6. How long have you lived there
7. I really like my new town
8. When I am older, I want to live in Boston

C Change each sentence to the kind named in ( ).
Write the new sentence.

9. It is hard to move to a new place. (interrogative)
10. Are there a lot of new students in your school? (declarative)
11. Meeting new friends does make things better. (interrogative)
12. Soon I will feel more at home. (interrogative)

Review and Assess

Write each sentence and add the correct end punctuation.

1. I play flute in the school orchestra
2. What instrument do you play
3. Is it hard to play the tuba
4. When I play the tuba, I often run out of breath
5. Do you practice often

Read each sentence. Write the letter of the word or the word and punctuation mark that complete each sentence.

6. Drums can be really _____

   A loud   C loud.
   B loud?   D Loud

7. _____ many years have you studied the piano?

   A What   C how
   B How?   D How

8. _____ play the clarinet.

   A I can   C can I
   B Can I   D I can?

9. Do you know how to play the _____

   A bass.   C Bass
   B bass   D bass?

10. I am not sure when the concert _____

   A starts   C starts?
   B starts.   D Starts

Varying Sentence Style

Different kinds of sentences can make your writing style exciting. Using questions in your personal narrative is one way to keep your readers interested.

- Have you been to a really great concert?
- What makes an outstanding concert?

A The personal narrative below has only declarative sentences. Rewrite the two underlined sentences as questions to make the paragraph more interesting.

1. <u>We should give a concert next week</u>. **2.** Mr. Jones can conduct the music. **3.** My brother can play harmonica. **4.** I wonder if your sister will be at the concert. **5.** We can have a short rehearsal before the concert. **6.** I will bring my violin. **7.** <u>You could make posters to invite our whole school</u>.

B Write your own interrogative sentence to begin this personal narrative.

_____ Everyone else in my family plays a musical instrument. I was worried that playing the guitar might be hard. After a few lessons, though, I was able to play a whole song. Was my family proud of me? You bet they were.

> **SENTENCE VARIETY**
>
> **Consider starting or ending your narrative with a question.**

C Write a brief personal narrative about hearing your favorite song. Vary your sentences to add style to your writing.

Imperative and Exclamatory Sentences

An **imperative sentence** gives a command or makes a request. It usually begins with a verb and ends with a period. The subject of an imperative sentence *(you)* is not shown, but it is understood. An **exclamatory sentence** shows strong feeling or surprise. Exclamatory sentences end with an exclamation mark.

Imperative sentence: Make a wish.
Exclamatory sentence: I had a wonderful birthday!

 A Read each sentence. Write **C** if the end punctuation is correct. Write **NC** if the end punctuation is not correct.

1. That is the biggest tamale I've ever seen. (exclamatory)
2. Mix the cornmeal carefully. (imperative)
3. Please hang up the piñata! (imperative)
4. I smashed that piñata to bits! (exclamatory)
5. Bring the presents outside! (imperative)

Read each sentence. Write the correct end punctuation.

6. I can't wait for my birthday party
7. Tell my friends they are all invited
8. Make sure they arrive on time
9. What great friends I have
10. I love a big party

B Write each sentence and add the correct end punctuation. Then write **I** if the sentence is imperative. Write **E** if the sentence is exclamatory.

   1. Blow out the candles
   2. What a beautiful present she gave you
   3. I can't believe how many gifts you have
   4. Make sure your guests have a good time
   5. That was a great party
   6. Boy, there's so much food left
   7. Please help me clean up
   8. Don't use that clean towel

C Write an imperative sentence and an exclamatory sentence for each event.

   9. visiting a museum
   10. going fishing
   11. playing a game
   12. cooking with your family

Review and Assess

Read each sentence. Write **E** if the sentence is exclamatory.
Write **I** if the sentence is imperative.

1. Look at the stars.
2. What a beautiful night!
3. I can't believe how many stars there are!
4. Tell me if you see a shooting star.
5. Make a wish on that star.

Write the letter of the answer that best completes the type of sentence in ( ).

6. _____ outside with me. (imperative)

    A My dog went   **C** Will you go
    B Eric wants to   **D** Come

7. Look at the _____ (imperative)

    A moon   **C** me.
    B moon.   **D** me!

8. It is so big and _____ (exclamatory)

    A bright.   **C** bright!
    B small.   **D** small?

9. _____ the brightest star. (imperative)

    A I like   **C** I see
    B I want   **D** Show me

10. I love the sparkling night _____ (exclamatory)

    A sky!   **C** I.
    B sky?   **D** sparkle.

Making Your Narrative Exciting

A command or an exclamation can make your audience want to read more. Using different sentence types helps give your writing a strong voice and an exciting style.

USE YOUR VOICE

A personal narrative is about *you*. Use exclamations to let your reader know how you feel.

- **Exclamatory:** You'll love reading about our giant family picnic!
- **Imperative:** Be sure to look at my pictures in the scrapbook.

A Add words to make the unfinished sentences exclamations.

1. There were many relatives at the picnic. **2.** In the morning the weather was perfect. **3.** I made cookies, and everyone else brought food too. **4.** People loved the _____! **5.** Suddenly, there was a crack of thunder and it started to pour. **6.** What a _____ there was! **7.** I still had a great time.

B Write an imperative sentence to begin this personal narrative. Then write an exclamation to make the paragraph more interesting to read. Hint: The command can be an invitation. The exclamation can describe how the meatballs taste.

8. _____ (command) **9.** My family and I make meatballs every Sunday. **10.** We mix the meat with spices and breadcrumbs. **11.** I love the way they smell as they cook. **12.** _____ (exclamation) **13.** Cooking with my family is one of my favorite things to do.

C Write a narrative paragraph for a postcard that tells about a picnic or a family event. Include one imperative sentence and one exclamatory sentence to make your narrative exciting.

Compound and Complex Sentences

A **simple sentence** expresses one complete thought. A **compound sentence** contains two simple sentences joined by a comma and a connecting word such as *and, but,* or *or.* A **complex sentence** contains a simple sentence combined with a group of words that cannot stand alone as a sentence.

Simple sentence: The young girl was scared.
Compound sentence: The young girl was scared, and she hugged her brother.
Complex sentence: When her brother cried, she held him tight.

A Read each sentence. Write **compound** if the sentence is a compound sentence. Write **complex** if the sentence is a complex sentence.

1. She looked outside, and she saw a fire.
2. As the fire neared, she began to worry.
3. She lifted her brother, and she carried him away.
4. The fire ended, but the girl was still afraid.
5. When her older brother came, she felt safe.

Read each sentence. Write **Yes** if the underlined words can stand alone to make a sentence. Write **No** if they cannot stand alone.

6. <u>The girl seemed calm</u>, but she was still upset.
7. <u>When the danger was over</u>, she began to relax.
8. Life on the prairie was hard, and <u>it was often lonely</u>.
9. The girl lived on a farm, but <u>she preferred the city</u>.
10. <u>After she moved to the farm</u>, she learned how to sew.

B Write the word you would use *(and, or,* or *but)* to join the following simple sentences to form compound sentences.

1. My brother is young. He is very strong.
2. I love my father. He loves me.
3. On weekends we go the park. We stay inside.
4. I don't mind staying inside. I prefer to go out.
5. I like the park. I enjoy seeing my friends there.

C Complete each sentence by adding a group of words from the box. Write each complete sentence and tell if it is **compound** or **complex**.

> Jenny likes games
> and sometimes she plays alone
> After she played with her dolls
> and she likes to build dollhouses
> Anna wants to build a dollhouse

6. Karen is a hard worker, _____.
7. _____, but she likes to play them outside.
8. When she gets older, _____.
9. Sometimes Nira plays with her friends, _____.
10. _____, Roberta took a nap.

Review and Assess

Write the word in ( ) that completes each sentence.

1. (After, But) finishing my chores, I ate breakfast.
2. I ate an egg, (since, and) I drank some milk.
3. I made eggs for my brother, (but, or) he did not eat them.
4. (Since, And) he was still hungry, I gave him cereal.
5. While he read a book, (and, I) washed the dishes.

Write the letter of the word that completes each sentence.

6. The birds sang, _____ then they flew away.

    A and   **C** since
    B or   **D** while

7. Was that a prairie dog, _____ was that a coyote?

    A since   **C** but
    B or   **D** while

8. I was looking for prairie dogs, _____ I couldn't find any.

    A since   **C** but
    B or   **D** while

9. _____ the sun began to set, I heard a pack of wolves.

    A And   **C** But
    B Or   **D** When

10. The wolves cried all night, _____ I was afraid.

    A and   **C** since
    B or   **D** soon

Combining Sentences

Using only simple sentences can make your narrative dull. Compound and complex sentences make writing smoother and more interesting.

- Firefighters are brave. They are careful. **(simple sentences)**
- Firefighters are brave, but they are careful. **(compound sentence)**
- Al smelled smoke. He raced outside. **(simple sentences)**
- When Al smelled smoke, he raced outside. **(complex sentence)**

A Combine each pair of sentences below, using the word in ( ). Remember to add a comma. Rewrite the paragraph.

1. Kenny smelled smoke. At first he didn't see any flames. (but)
2. Then he saw a small fire in the neighbors' yard. He ran outside. (so)
3. Kenny could get out the hose. He could call the fire department. (or)
4. He was careful. He remembered to stay calm. (and) **5.** He called 911. The fire truck was there in three minutes to put out the fire. (and)
6. The neighbors invited him over for pizza. He had had enough excitement for one day. (but)

B Complete the sentences below by making them compound or complex sentences. Write the new sentences. The first one is done for you.

7. When his parents were entertaining friends in the basement, Marco was a little afraid upstairs. **8.** The noises outside frightened him because _____. **9.** When he saw shadows, _____. **10.** He knew he could run downstairs, but _____. Then he got a bright idea. He turned on all the lights. **11.** Marco fell asleep before _____.

C Write a short personal narrative about something that scared you. Use different types of sentences to make your writing come alive.

Writing a Personal Narrative

A **test** may ask you to write a personal narrative. Your narrative should have a beginning, middle, and end. Use clue words such as *once* and *now* to show the order of events. Follow the tips below.

USE *I* AND *ME*

A personal narrative is a story about your experiences. Tell your story using *I* and *me*.

Understand the prompt. Make sure you know what to do. Read the prompt carefully. A test prompt for a personal narrative could look like this:

> **Think about an exciting experience or event in your life that you would like to share. Write a personal narrative about it. Consider creating a mood of suspense, humor, or fantasy.**

Key words and phrases are *experience, event in your life,* and *personal narrative.*

Find a good topic. Use your memory. Think about events or experiences that you remember. Use photos, diaries, and scrapbooks to help you get ideas.

Organize your ideas. Write notes for the narrative on scratch paper.

Possible Title: The Kite and the Tree

Summary

What Happened? Went kite flying with Amy and Mom
When? Last Saturday   **Where?** The park
Beginning: My mom agreed to take me to fly a kite.
Middle: The kite got caught in a tree.
End: We gave up. Mom said she would get me another kite.

Write a good beginning. Write a snappy first sentence.

Develop and elaborate ideas. Use your notes to help organize the events. Make sure events flow smoothly and are in the correct order.

Write a strong ending. Describe how you felt about the events.

Check your work. Add vivid words to make your voice strong.

See how the personal narrative below addresses the prompt, flows from the beginning to the middle to the end, and strongly expresses the writer's voice.

1 —— Last Saturday was a perfect day to fly a kite! I just couldn't wait to get to the park on this warm, windy day. Mom agreed to take me there, along with my best friend, Amy.

3 —— After we got to the park, Amy held the kite high. Then she let it go as I began running wildly. The kite darted around as I furiously unrolled the string. Then the wind lifted the kite. It almost seemed like the kite could touch the clouds. —— 2

4 —— Amy wanted to fly the kite, and I gave her the string. At first, she was smiling as the kite sailed through the sky. Suddenly the wind died down, and the kite began to dive. Then the kite got caught in a tree. No matter what we did, we could not get it down. Amy looked really sad, but I told her not to worry. I could get a new kite, but good friends are much harder to get. —— 5

1. The first sentence grabs the reader's attention.
2. Vivid words strengthen the writer's voice.
3. The writer clearly shows the order of events.
4. Compound sentences make the writing more interesting.
5. This strong ending shows the writer's feelings about friendship.

Nouns

A **noun** is a word that names a person, place, or thing. A **common noun** names any person, place, or thing.

Persons: My **sister** wants to be a **zookeeper**.
Places: She often visits the **zoo** in the **city**.
Things: We take the **subway** and bring a **camera**.

A One of the underlined words in each sentence is a noun. Write that noun.

1. The mouse <u>darted</u> across the <u>floor</u>.
2. He heard a noise <u>from</u> a <u>shelf</u>.
3. It was a cricket with two <u>shiny</u> black <u>eyes</u>.
4. He once had <u>lived</u> in the <u>country</u> near a brook.
5. Both creatures were <u>looking</u> for a <u>friend</u>.

Each sentence has two nouns. One is underlined. Write the other noun in each sentence.

6. The <u>cricket</u> slept in a matchbox.
7. A huge <u>cat</u> was switching its tail.
8. He was a <u>friend</u>, not an enemy.
9. The <u>city</u> was not a quiet place.
10. The <u>smell</u> of food made him hungry.
11. He ate a piece of <u>liverwurst</u>.
12. The meal made the <u>friends</u> feel better.

B Write the three nouns in each sentence.

1. The cricket jumped on a pile of magazines.
2. In the meadow were bullfrogs and snakes.
3. His home was in a tree near a brook.
4. There were no subways, sidewalks, or newsstands.
5. The mouse climbed through the pipe in the dark.
6. The street was full of the sounds of traffic.
7. There were many lights, colors, and noises.
8. The author of this story has won many awards.

C Add a noun from the box that makes sense to complete each sentence. Write the sentences.

chirps	stores	information
creatures	evenings	bowl

9. Crickets are amazing _____. **10.** On warm summer _____ you can hear them. **11.** Their _____ are like odd music. **12.** Many pet _____ sell them, and they are easy to raise. **13.** They can live in a glass _____. **14.** Be sure to find _____ about what they need.

Review and Assess

Write the sentences. Underline all the nouns in each sentence.

1. The insect made noise with its wings.
2. The friends stopped for lunch in the city.
3. There were many lights and people in the street.
4. Each night, she makes a wish on the brightest star.
5. He rode the train one day with his sister.
6. Let's eat sandwiches, apples, and pie for lunch.

Read each sentence. Write the letter of the word that is a noun.

7. When I was only five, my family went to New York.

   A When   **C** family

   B only   **D** went

8. We used the subway instead of taking taxicabs.

   A used   **C** taking

   B instead   **D** taxicabs

9. Many travelers ride trains every day.

   A Many   **C** ride

   B travelers   **D** every

10. Many people get along without cars.

    A people   **C** get

    B along   **D** without

UNIT 2 FOCUS ON WRITING A DESCRIPTION

Using Exact Common Nouns in Descriptions

Exact nouns are powerful writing tools. Look at the nouns in the first sentence below. See how exact nouns make the new sentence more vivid.

- The dog barked at the bug on the flower.
- The poodle barked at the cricket on the tulip.

A Improve the paragraph below by replacing the underlined words with words from the box. Write the new sentences.

seals	fish	lemonade
trainers	roars	picnic

1. I like to watch the <u>animals</u> at the zoo. **2.** At noon, you can see <u>guys</u> feed them. **3.** The seals leap up to catch <u>food</u> that someone tosses. **4.** Sometimes we take a <u>meal</u> to the zoo park. **5.** We bring sandwiches and <u>drinks</u>. **6.** While we eat, we can hear the <u>sounds</u> of lions.

B Replace each underlined word with a more exact noun of your own. Rewrite the new sentences.

7. There were many <u>things</u> on the playground.
8. <u>Stuff</u> littered the ground.
9. You could hear the <u>sounds</u> of dogs.

EXACT NOUNS

In your writing, replace words such as *things* and *stuff* with exact nouns.

C Describe your favorite place outside. Use exact nouns to make your description vivid.

Proper Nouns

A **proper noun** names a particular person, place, or thing. The words *George, New Mexico,* and *Monday* are proper nouns. Begin proper nouns with capital letters.

Nouns that are not proper nouns are called **common nouns.** The words *boy, state,* and *day* are common nouns. Note how the common nouns in the first sentence below are replaced by proper nouns in the second sentence.

- I saw a <u>girl</u> in the <u>park</u>.
- I saw <u>Juanita</u> in <u>Griffith Park</u>.

A One of the underlined words or groups of words in each sentence is a proper noun. Write that proper noun.

    1. <u>Mr. Morales</u> is taking my class on a field <u>trip</u>. **2.** He is my <u>teacher</u> at <u>Burbank Middle School</u>. **3.** <u>We</u> are going to visit the <u>Natural History Museum</u>. **4.** My best <u>friend</u> at school is <u>Robert Ruíz</u>. **5.** Next <u>week</u> our class will go to the <u>Getty Museum</u>.

Write the sentences. Underline all the proper nouns in each sentence.

    6. José Torres lives down the street from the Mayfair Gardens. **7.** He works in the garden every Saturday and Sunday. **8.** Betty, Henry, and Alphonso like to help him plant flowers and vegetables. **9.** Their hard work helps to make Los Angeles a nice place to live. **10.** Senator Beakins, who lives on Taft Avenue, always waves when he walks by.

B Replace the underlined word or words in each sentence with a proper noun from the box. Write the new sentences.

January	Mrs. Green
North Broadway	Pacific Ocean
Mark Alvarez	City Hall

1. <u>He</u> is my best friend.
2. I met him last <u>month</u>.
3. We met in front of <u>a building</u>.
4. We both live on <u>a big street</u>.
5. <u>A woman</u> takes us to school every day.
6. On weekends we go fishing in the <u>water</u>.

C Write a proper noun to complete each sentence.

7. My name is _____.
8. My best friend is _____.
9. The name of my favorite sports team is _____.
10. My school is called _____.
11. I live in _____.
12. My favorite singer is _____.

Review and Assess

Write each underlined word or words. Write **P** next to each proper noun and **C** next to each common noun.

1. <u>Julie</u> is my best <u>friend</u>.
2. Julie has an older <u>sister</u> named <u>Stacey</u>.
3. Stacey is a <u>center</u> on the <u>Flying Eagles</u> soccer team.
4. Stacey practices every <u>Saturday</u> with her <u>coach</u>, Mr. White.
5. Their next <u>game</u> will be at <u>Big Bear Lake</u>.

Write the letter of the words or word that is a proper noun.

6. Mary is a volunteer at the local community center.

   A Mary   **C** volunteer
   B local   **D** community center

7. She works on Monday night and during the weekend.

   A She   **C** Monday
   B night   **D** weekend

8. She likes to read stories to Mrs. Martens.

   A She   **C** read
   B stories   **D** Mrs. Martens

9. Last week, Senator Brown came to the center.

   A Last   **C** week
   B Senator Brown **D** center

10. He gave a speech about plans to improve Grand Avenue.

   A He   **C** speech
   B plans   **D** Grand Avenue

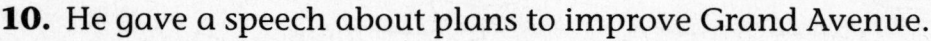

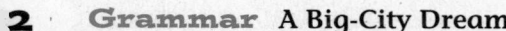

Using Proper Nouns in Descriptions

Proper nouns make your description clear. Read the nouns in the first sentence below. See how proper nouns make the second sentence clear.

- He lives in a city.
- Mr. Cohn lives in Denver.

A Complete each sentence below with a proper noun from the list. Write the new sentences.

> **PROPER NOUNS**
>
> **Check to see if adding proper nouns would make your writing clearer.**

Monday	Tigers
World Series	Mr. Drake
Fair Oaks County	

1. _____ is my favorite teacher. **2.** I think he is the best teacher in _____. **3.** I can't wait for class to begin each _____. **4.** Mr. Drake is also the coach of our school's baseball team, the _____. **5.** Last year they made it to the state _____.

B Replace the underlined words with a proper noun to make each sentence clear. Write the new sentences.

6. My family and I live near <u>the river</u>.
7. I go swimming there with <u>my best friend</u>.
8. Sometimes we go to <u>the park</u>.
9. Can we help <u>my neighbor</u> with chores?

C Write a short description of your community. Tell about people who live there and places you like to visit. Include proper nouns to make your description clear.

Regular Plural Nouns

Nouns that name one person, place, or thing are **singular nouns.**
Plural nouns name more than one person, place, or thing. Add **-s**
to form the plural of most nouns. Add **-es** to form the plural of nouns
that end in **ch, sh, s, ss,** or **x.** To form the plural of nouns that end
in a **consonant** and a **y,** change the **y** to **i** and add **-es.**

bird/birds	bush/bushes	butterfly/butterflies
dog/dogs	dress/dresses	family/families
ferret/ferrets	fox/foxes	party/parties
monkey/monkeys	gas/gases	pony/ponies
snake/snakes	lunch/lunches	puppy/puppies

 A Write the plural noun in each sentence.

1. Jerry's hamster eats carrots.
2. Our dog likes to chase squirrels.
3. My gerbil had babies last week.
4. The foxes sleep in a den.
5. My aunt has many pets.

Write each singular noun as a plural noun.

6. beetle
7. spider
8. walrus
9. penny
10. bunny
11. bunch

B Write the plural form of the underlined noun or nouns in each sentence.

1. Look at the little <u>bunny</u> in the <u>cage</u>.
2. See its fluffy <u>tail</u>.
3. I like to play a <u>game</u> with it.
4. I place a <u>carrot</u> behind its <u>back</u>.
5. I look at my <u>watch</u>.
6. Then I time how long it takes it to eat the <u>treat</u>.

C Write two plural nouns that name what you might find in each place.

7. a zoo
8. a kitchen
9. a school
10. a garage
11. a museum
12. a closet
13. a mall
14. a playground

Review and Assess

Change the underlined noun in each sentence to a plural noun.
Write the new sentences.

1. Why did the <u>frog</u> jump into the pond?
2. The <u>lizard</u> sat on the rock.
3. Three cats sipped from the <u>dish</u>.
4. Those rabbits hopped across the <u>ditch</u>.
5. The <u>butterfly</u> landed on the grass.

Read each sentence. Write the letter of the correct plural form
that completes each sentence.

6. Some _____ sleep all day.

    A gerbils   **C** gerbiles

    B gerbil's   **D** gerbils'

7. My gerbil, Theo, has two water _____.

    A dishs   **C** dishses

    B dishes   **D** dish's

8. Last week, Theo ran after a group of _____.

    A ladyses   **C** ladys

    B ladyes   **D** ladies

9. One lady said that Theo was faster than two _____.

    A fox's   **C** foxes

    B foxs   **D** foxses

10. Another lady gave Theo two _____.

    A treats   **C** treatss

    B treates   **D** treatz

Using Plural Nouns in Descriptions

Spell plural nouns correctly in your descriptions.
Give readers word pictures about these plural nouns.

FORM PLURALS
Do not add an apostrophe to indicate a plural noun. No: *My dog's bark.* Yes: *My dogs bark.*

- **No:** Three monkies ate bananas in the zoo.
- **Yes:** Three noisy monkeys ate bananas in the zoo.

A Write the plural form of each underlined noun.
Add a word from the box to describe each noun. Write the new sentences.

wooden   spotted   yellow   sunny   sleepy

1. Two bright _____ <u>bus</u> took our class to the zoo.
2. We saw _____ <u>leopard</u> pace in their cages.
3. Lions warmed themselves on the _____ <u>rock</u>.
4. Mothers pushed _____ <u>baby</u> in strollers.
5. Later we sat on hard _____ <u>bench</u> for a picnic.

B Write the correct plural of each underlined noun. Add your own
word to describe each plural noun. Write the new paragraph.

  6. When I was nine, Aunt Bea gave me two _____ <u>bunny</u>.
7. They were only _____ <u>inch</u> long. 8. Soon they ate lettuce
and _____ <u>strawberry</u>. 9. Now I groom them with _____ <u>brush</u>.
10. I keep their _____ <u>bowl</u> full of food and water. 11. They have
_____ <u>eye</u> and healthy fur.

C Write a short description of monkeys that you have seen in a zoo,
in books, or on television. Use at least two plural nouns.

Irregular Plural Nouns

Some plural forms of nouns do not end in **-s** or **-es.** To form these **irregular plurals,** you may have to change the spelling of the word. Study the irregular plural nouns underlined below.

calf/calves	leaf/leaves	ox/oxen	tooth/teeth
child/children	life/lives	person/people	wife/wives
foot/feet	loaf/loaves	scarf/scarves	wolf/wolves
goose/geese	man/men	self/selves	woman/women
hoof/hooves	mouse/mice	shelf/shelves	

Some nouns have the same form for both singular and plural.

deer/deer	moose/moose	sheep/sheep	trout/trout

 A Write the irregular plural noun in each sentence.

1. The children walked down to the creek.
2. As the girls walked, three mice ran across their path.
3. There were no other people around.
4. Then all the animals ran into the leaves.
5. Two moose walked across the path a minute later.
6. Later, Aliza baked three loaves of bread.
7. Sally dusted the shelves.
8. Pat herded the cows and sheep home.

B A plural noun is underlined in each sentence. Write **C** if the plural noun is correct. If it is not correct, write the correct form.

1. Claire and Ana are happy young <u>woman</u>.
2. Ana likes to watch the <u>trout</u> in the pond.
3. Claire tells Ana a joke about <u>wolfs</u>.
4. Claire stamps her <u>feet</u> as she laughs.
5. Everyone likes these <u>person</u>.

C Complete each sentence with the plural form of a noun in the box. Write the sentences.

wolf	leaf	life	goose
foot	moose	child	

6. Ever since they were _____, Claire and Ana have lived in the country. 7. They spend their _____ surrounded by animals. 8. Claire loves to watch gray _____ run. 9. Ana likes _____ with large antlers. 10. In the forest, the girls take off their shoes and dip their _____ into the pond. 11. They collect _____ from the trees. 12. Both girls watch the _____ fly in the sky.

Review and Assess

A plural noun is underlined in each sentence. Write **C** if the plural noun is correct. If it is not correct, write the correct form.

1. Dina keeps her <u>mices</u> in a cage.
2. She loves every animal, even <u>moose</u>!
3. She wears <u>scarfs</u> when it is cold outside.
4. Dina has to go outside to clean the cow's <u>hoofs</u>.
5. She milks her three <u>sheep</u> each morning.

Write the letter of the word that correctly completes each sentence.

6. Doris fed the _____ warm milk.

    A deers   **C** mooses
    B calfs   **D** calves

7. She saw two _____ run across the path.

    A deer   **C** deers
    B child   **D** childs

8. Two big _____ snorted in the barn.

    A ox   **C** oxen
    B goose   **D** feet

9. The three _____ at the stables help her clean stalls.

    A child   **C** woman
    B men   **D** wife

10. Doris feeds the horses _____ of bread.

    A loaves   **C** leaf
    B lifes   **D** loafs

Using Irregular Plural Nouns in Descriptions

A good description helps readers "see" what you are writing about. When you use irregular plural nouns in your descriptions, be sure to spell them correctly.

- **No:** The sheeps all stood together.
- **Yes:** The fluffy, white sheep all stood together.

> **USING YOUR SENSES**
>
> **Use vivid words to paint pictures for your reader. What does something look, sound, or taste like?**

A Write the plural form of each underlined noun. Add a word from the box to describe each noun. Write the new sentences.

| three | wool | dry | graceful | sleepy |

1. It was cold, so we wore many _____ scarf.
2. We heard _____ leaf rustling under our feet.
3. Soon we passed _____ woman dragging firewood.
4. They carried their _____ child on their backs.
5. Suddenly, two _____ deer leaped across the path.

B Write the plural form of each underlined noun. Add your own word to describe each plural noun. Write the new paragraph.

6. The _____ child couldn't wait to get to the pond. 7. They ran down the path as fast as their _____ foot could take them. 8. On the way, they saw a huge flock of _____ goose flying overhead. 9. When they got to the pond, they shared two _____ loaf of bread for lunch. 10. Then they swam in the pond with the _____ trout.

C Write a description of a trip through the woods. Describe one of the following animals: wolves, geese, sheep, mice, or deer.

Possessive Nouns

A **possessive noun** is a noun that shows who owns, or possesses, something.

Use the following rules to form possessive nouns.

- Add an **apostrophe (')** and **-s** to a **singular noun**.
  the **lizard's** claw   the **reptile's** skin   the **mother's** eggs

- Add an **apostrophe (')** to a **plural noun** that ends in **-s**.
  the **parents'** nest   the **insects'** tongues   the **dragons'** teeth

- Add an **apostrophe (')** and **-s** to a **plural noun** that does not end in **-s**.
  three **deer's** eyes   the **people's** hope   the **oxen's** ears

A Choose the correct possessive noun to complete each sentence. Write the possessive nouns you choose.

1. The (snakes, snake's) eyes were green.
2. During the day, it lay in the (sun's, suns') rays.
3. The snake hissed at three (hawk's, hawks') nests.
4. Most (reptile's, reptiles') skins are cold and scaly.
5. The (cobra's, cobras') tongue darted out.

Write each noun below as a possessive noun.

6. animal
7. desert
8. mice
9. adults
10. woman

B Change each underlined noun to a possessive noun to complete each sentence. Write the sentences.

1. The <u>island</u> beach is white and smooth.
2. All the <u>residents</u> boats are tied to the pier.
3. Many <u>trees</u> leaves sway gently in the wind.
4. The <u>women</u> clothes are drying in the sun.
5. Children like to play near the <u>lifeguard</u> chair.

C Write a possessive noun of your own to complete each sentence.

6. Some _____ eyes are brown.
7. A _____ tail can be very long.
8. Many _____ nests are high up in the trees.
9. Did you know that _____ teeth are very sharp?
10. The _____ eyes closed as they went to sleep.
11. Be careful of that _____ claws!
12. We found fourteen _____ eggs.

Review and Assess

Write each word as a possessive noun.

1. claw
2. hunters
3. alligator
4. fly
5. men

Write the letter of the word that completes each sentence.

6. The _____ claws are used to dig holes.

   A dragon   **C** dragons
   B dragon's   **D** dragons's

7. _____ tongues are used to smell things.

   A Snake'   **C** Snakes'
   B Snake's   **D** Snakes's

8. That _____ skin is hard and scaly.

   A beasts   **C** beasts'
   B beasts's   **D** beast's

9. Their _____ ridges are good for biting.

   A teeth's   **C** teeths'
   B tooths'   **D** tooths's

10. The _____ spots help him hide from other animals.

    A baby's   **C** babys'
    B babie's   **D** babies's

Using Possessive Nouns in Descriptions

Possessive nouns can make your writing less wordy. Notice how adding a possessive noun makes your sentences sound smoother.

> **SMOOTH WRITING**
>
> **Using possessive nouns can make your writing sound better.**

- The <u>sister of the girl</u> studies North American birds.
- The <u>girl's sister</u> studies North American birds.

A Make each sentence less wordy by replacing the underlined words with a possessive noun phrase. Write the new sentences.

1. <u>The friend of my brother</u> works in the Sonora Desert. **2.** His white hat protects him from the <u>rays of the sun</u>. **3.** <u>The work that Michael does</u> is a lot of fun. **4.** Michael takes <u>groups of children</u> on nature walks through the desert. **5.** Yesterday they saw <u>the nests of three hawks</u>.

B Add your own possessive noun to complete each sentence. Write the sentence.

6. My best _____ name is Mary. **7.** _____ favorite place to visit is the desert. **8.** We like to go there in her _____ car. **9.** She showed me some _____ footprints in the sand. **10.** Once we found a _____ bones near a cactus.

C Write a short description of someone you know. Include at least two possessive nouns. Check your writing to make sure that there are no unnecessary words.

Writing a Description

TIMED TESTS

**Budget your time.
Here's how to
spend your time on
a 45-minute test.
PLAN: 10 minutes
WRITE: 25 minutes
CHECK: 10 minutes**

A **test** may ask you to write a description. Use vivid
sense words to make your writing lively. Follow the
tips below.

Understand the prompt. Make sure you know
what to do. A prompt for a description could look
like this:

> **Write a description of a person who is special to you.
> Help readers use their senses to picture this person.**

Key words and phrases are *description, person who is special,* and *senses.*

Find a good topic. Pick someone you know enough about to write
a good description. Consider a relative, neighbor, friend, or teacher.

Organize your ideas. For this assignment, you could make a
description web on scratch paper. Write the name of your topic in
the center circle. Write details about that person in connected circles.

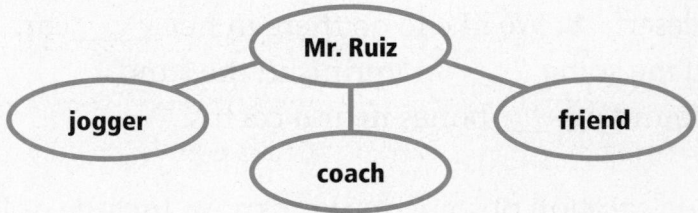

Write a good beginning. With a good start, you're halfway there.
A strong topic sentence can "set up" your entire piece.

Develop and elaborate ideas. Use the subject and details in your web. Don't forget to use words that appeal to the senses.

Write a strong ending. Try to make the ending interesting.

Check your work. Make any necessary changes.

See how the description below addresses the prompt, has a strong beginning and end, and uses details that appeal to the senses.

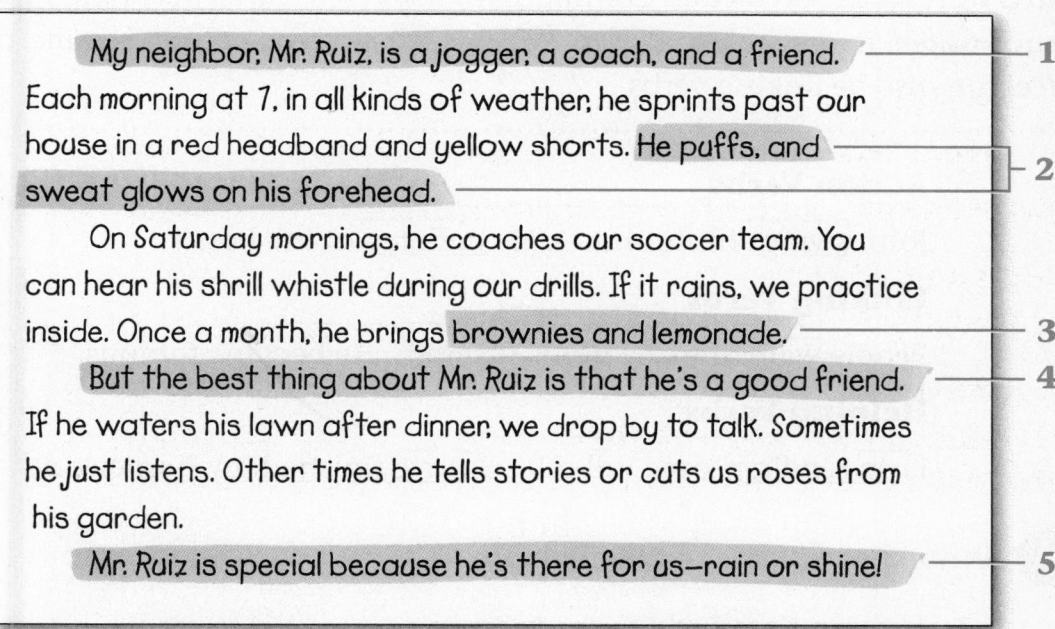

My neighbor, Mr. Ruiz, is a jogger, a coach, and a friend. —— 1
Each morning at 7, in all kinds of weather, he sprints past our
house in a red headband and yellow shorts. He puffs, and
sweat glows on his forehead. —— 2

On Saturday mornings, he coaches our soccer team. You
can hear his shrill whistle during our drills. If it rains, we practice
inside. Once a month, he brings brownies and lemonade. —— 3

But the best thing about Mr. Ruiz is that he's a good friend. —— 4
If he waters his lawn after dinner, we drop by to talk. Sometimes
he just listens. Other times he tells stories or cuts us roses from
his garden.

Mr. Ruiz is special because he's there for us—rain or shine! —— 5

1. The first sentence organizes the entire piece.
2. There is a strong appeal to the senses.
3. Specific nouns give details.
4. Description builds up to the most important quality.
5. This strong ending is based on earlier sentences.

Verbs

You have learned that sentences have a subject and a predicate. The main word in the predicate is a **verb.** Sometimes a **helping verb** comes before the main verb.

Action verbs are words that show what someone or something does. **Linking verbs** do not show action. Instead, they link, or join, the subject to a word in the predicate. Common linking verbs use forms of the verb **be,** such as *am, is, are, was,* and *were.* Words such as *seem, appear, become,* and *feel* can also be linking verbs.

Action Verbs

John <u>swings</u> his hammer. He <u>hollered</u> at the boss.

Linking Verbs

People <u>were</u> amazed at his strength. He <u>became</u> famous.

Helping Verbs

I <u>am reading</u> some tall tales. I <u>have finished</u> my homework.

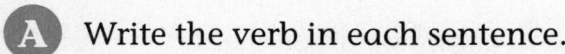 **A** Write the verb in each sentence.

1. The sun rises early in the morning.
2. At noon the sun is directly overhead.
3. The sun sets at the end of the day.
4. Later, the moon appears in the sky.
5. Wolves howl at the full moon.
6. Miners work very hard.
7. They build strong muscles.
8. The mines are often dark and damp.
9. Some miners drill deep below the ground.

B Use each noun below to write two sentences. Use an action verb in the first sentence. Use a linking verb in the second sentence.

1. **man (Action verb):** _____
2. **man (Linking verb):** _____
3. **rocks (Action verb):** _____
4. **rocks (Linking verb):** _____

C Find four more verbs hidden in the group of letters. Use the verbs you find to complete each sentence below. Write the sentences. The first sentence has been done for you.

J	B	I	S	S
S	L	T	S	A
D	A	D	W	N
H	S	Z	U	G
R	T	N	N	G
H	E	Q	G	S
F	D	H	R	M
L	W	E	R	E

5. The crew **dug** the tunnel.
6. They _____ a boulder in front of the entrance.
7. They _____ their hammers in rhythm with each other.
8. Together they _____ a loud song.
9. How tired and cold they _____!

Review and Assess

Write the verb in each sentence. Circle the verb if it is an action verb.
Underline the verb if it is a linking verb.

1. The baby cries during the night.
2. His cries are so loud.
3. He is a big, handsome baby.
4. He laughs out loud at the dog.
5. Everybody smiles at the baby.

Write the letter of the word that completes each sentence.

6. Chidi _____ his father during the summer.

   A from   **C** be
   B are   **D** helped

7. He _____ a swimming pool.

   A built   **C** cry
   B love   **D** are

8. Then he _____ down some trees.

   A has   **C** be
   B was   **D** chopped

9. He _____ the strongest boy around.

   A am   **C** are
   B was   **D** be

10. The people in the town _____ glad to see him.

    A is   **C** were
    B happy   **D** run

Replacing Forms of *Be* with Action Verbs

Sometimes you can make your writing stronger by replacing linking verbs *(am, is, are, was, were)* with action verbs. In the examples below, the phrase with the linking verb has been replaced by an action verb to present a clearer picture for readers.

- I <u>was cold</u>.   The boulder <u>was shiny</u>.   **Linking Verbs**
- I <u>shivered</u>.   The boulder <u>sparkled</u>.   **Action Verbs**

A Each underlined phrase contains a linking verb. Replace the phrase in each sentence with one of these action words: *shimmers, sweated, yelled, scowls, smiled, trembles.*

1. His boss <u>is afraid</u>.
2. Every worker <u>is angry</u> at the news.
3. The sun <u>is bright</u> in the sky.
4. The miners <u>were hot</u> as they worked.
5. They <u>were loud</u> when they used the noisy drills.
6. After they finished work, they <u>were happy</u>.

B Choose two places from column one. Write four sentences that compare and contrast these places. Use verbs from column two.

classroom	write, paint, add, listen, speak
gym	bounce, climb, jump, race, laugh
auditorium	listen, clap, laugh, sing, perform
playground	climb, race, shout, throw, skip

C Write a paragraph that compares and contrasts two sports or activities. Include action verbs to make likenesses and differences clear.

Verbs in Sentences

The subject and the verb in a sentence must work together, or **agree.** Decide whether a noun subject is singular or plural. Then use the verb form that agrees with it: Marven laughs. The lumberjacks laugh. If the verb tells what the subject is or does now (present tense), follow the rules below.

- When a singular noun or *he, she,* or *it* is the subject, the verb usually is written with **-s** or **-es:** The snow falls gently. She watches a skier.
- Verbs that end in a **consonant** and **y** change the **y** to **i** before adding **-es:** The skier flies through the snow.
- When the singular pronoun *I* or *you* is the subject, write the verb without **-s** or **-es:** I fall asleep. You watch a skier.
- When a plural noun or a plural pronoun *(we, you, they)* is the subject, write the verb without **-s** or **-es:** The snowflakes dart through the air. Then they stick to the ground.
- For the verb **be,** use *is* to agree with singular subjects and *are* to agree with plural subjects: The snow is white and cold. My friends are happy when it snows.

 Write **Yes** if the underlined verb in each sentence agrees with the subject. Write **No** if the verb and subject do not agree.

1. I sees the snowy mountains in the distance.
2. Four peaks shine in the sunlight.
3. This valley glows at dusk.
4. Grizzly bears tramps through the snow.
5. A grizzly cub cries for its mother.

B Put each group of words in order and write a complete sentence. Make sure the verb agrees with the subject. Remember to begin sentences with a capital letter and end them with a period.

1. boy eat breakfast the
2. gobbles muffins eggs he and
3. brother toast make his always
4. they outside then runs
5. at throw his snowballs brother he

C Make up your own sentences, using the words given. Use the correct form of the verb to agree with each subject.

6. freeze
7. growl
8. be
9. cry
10. whisper
11. grab
12. laugh
13. tremble

Grammar Marven of the Great North Woods   **73**

Review and Assess

Choose the correct verb to complete each sentence. Write the sentence.

1. The lumberjack (wake, wakes) up before sunrise.
2. His eyes (is, are) blue and clear.
3. He (pull, pulls) on his socks and pants.
4. His stomach (growl, growls) loudly.
5. The cook (fry, fries) eggs and ham for everyone.

Write the letter of the word that completes each sentence.

6. The young boy _____ a deep growl.

   A hear   **C** hears
   B is   **D** are

7. He _____ frightened by the sound.

   A is   **C** are
   B be   **D** tries

8. Trees _____ in the strong wind.

   A is   **C** shakes
   B sway   **D** sways

9. He _____ to find his way in the storm.

   A try   **C** trys
   B trie   **D** tries

10. Suddenly he _____ his friend behind the trees.

   A be   **C** see
   B sees   **D** am

Using Verbs in Comparisons

You can use vivid verbs to make comparisons. A **simile** is a comparison between two unlike things using the words *like* or *as*. The example below shows how adding a strong verb and a simile can strengthen a sentence.

- Martín's eyes are bright.
- Martín's eyes glitter like stars.

A Complete the comparisons with one of the following words or phrases: *silver dollar, siren, diamonds, ghosts, pigs.*

1. The ice <u>glistens</u> like _____.
2. Those lumberjacks <u>grunt</u> like _____.
3. Shadows <u>slide</u> across the room like _____.
4. A full moon <u>glows</u> like a _____.
5. The wounded calf <u>wails</u> like a _____.

> **SIMILES**
>
> **You can get ideas for similes by picturing how animals look or act.**

B Complete each sentence by adding a subject and a simile. Use your own words or the following words for your similes: *lion, deer, bird, leaf, tornado.* Make sure subjects and verbs agree.

Example: <u>She</u> runs like a <u>cheetah</u>.

6. _____ shakes like a _____.
7. _____ spins like a _____.
8. _____ leap like _____.
9. _____ sings like a _____.
10. _____ roars like a _____.

C Write a paragraph that compares and contrasts two games or playground activities. Use your own verbs and similes or ones that appear on this page. Make sure each subject agrees with its verb.

Verb Tenses: Present, Past, and Future

The **tense** of a verb tells *when* something happens. A verb in the **present tense** shows action that is happening now. A verb in the **past tense** shows action that has already happened. Verbs in the past tense often end in **-ed.** A verb in the **future tense** shows action that will happen. Use the helping verb *will* to form verbs in the future tense.

Present Tense: Emily <u>works</u> on a ranch.
Past Tense: Emily <u>worked</u> on a ranch.
Future Tense: Emily <u>will work</u> on a ranch.

A Write **Present, Past,** or **Future** to tell the tense of each underlined verb.

1. Emily <u>lives</u> in the United States.
2. Last summer she <u>visited</u> a ranch in Argentina.
3. She <u>learned</u> about many different animals.
4. She <u>wants</u> to learn more about horses.
5. Next year, her whole family <u>will visit</u> the ranch.

Write the verb in each sentence. Circle the verbs in the past tense. Underline the verbs in the future tense.

6. Erin loves horses.
7. She brushed their coats each morning.
8. Then she trimmed their hooves.
9. She braids their manes and tails each week.
10. Soon she will get a new horse.

B Rewrite the sentences by changing each underlined verb to the past tense.

1. Juan <u>rounds</u> up the cattle.
2. He <u>moves</u> them from one pasture to another.
3. Sometimes he <u>yells</u> to make them run.
4. Some cattle <u>refuse</u> to move.
5. Then he <u>will scream</u> even louder.

C Rewrite each sentence twice. First, write the sentence by changing the underlined verb to the past tense. Then write the sentence by changing the underlined verb to the future tense.

6. Karen <u>cooks</u> lunch at noon.
7. All her relatives <u>like</u> her cooking.
8. She <u>washes</u> the dishes after lunch.
9. After lunch, Karen <u>walks</u> around the ranch.
10. In July, her friend Luz <u>visits</u>.
11. Luz <u>enjoys</u> her friend's cooking.

Review and Assess

Choose the correct tense of the verb shown in ( ). Write the sentence.

1. Today many people (work, worked) on farms in Argentina.
2. We (call, will call) the citizens of this country Argentines.
3. Now many farmers (produced, produce) wheat and corn.
4. Next year, farmers (raised, will raise) more cattle than ever before.
5. Last year more than 35 million people (lived, will live) in Argentina.

Write the letter of the word or words that complete each sentence.

6. Yesterday I _____ a ranch.

   A visit   **C** visited
   B will visit **D** visits

7. My sister _____ on the ranch every day.

   A play   **C** player
   B plays **D** playing

8. Next week I _____ my cousin in Toledo.

   A calls   **C** called
   B will calls **D** will call

9. She always _____ my calls.

   A enjoy   **C** enjoys
   B enjoying **D** will enjoy

10. My parents _____ to see her last week.

   A hoping **C** hopes
   B hoped   **D** will hope

Using Correct Verb Tenses in Your Writing

Good writers choose their words carefully. They use
lively verbs and tenses that show the right time.

VERB CHOICE
Short verbs *(lift)* are often more effective than long ones *(elevate)*.

- When I was young, I <u>trotted</u> around the ring
  on my pony. Now I <u>gallop</u> along the trails on
  my horse. Next week, we <u>will jump</u> the hurdles.

A Replace each underlined word with a verb from the box.
Write the new paragraph. Make sure you use the correct tense.

race	haul	dream	hope	spray

1. Last year, I <u>thought</u> about being a cowboy. **2.** Now I <u>want</u>
to be a firefighter. **3.** When I am a firefighter, I will <u>carry</u> heavy
hoses up a ladder. **4.** I will <u>put</u> water on the flames. **5.** I can't
wait to <u>go</u> into buildings and save people.

B Add a vivid verb of your own to complete each sentence.
Make sure you use the correct tense.

6. Two summers ago my family _____ Chicago. **7.** My sister
and I _____ in Grant Park. **8.** The taxis _____ down the street faster
than the cars back home. **9.** Fruit sellers _____, "Apples, grapes,
bananas." **10.** We _____ in Lake Michigan. **11.** Next summer,
I _____ to go back.

C Write a letter to a friend that compares and contrasts things you
liked to do when you were young and what you like to do now.
Choose your verb tenses carefully.

Using Correct Verb Tenses

- To form the **present tense** of most verbs, add **-s** or **-es** if the subject is a singular noun or *he, she,* or *it:* The storm <u>approaches</u>. It <u>grows</u> dark. Do not add an ending to the verb if the subject is *I, you,* or plural: I <u>run</u> for shelter. Clouds <u>gather</u>.
- To form the **past tense** of most verbs, add **-ed:** It <u>rained</u>.
- For most one-syllable verbs that end in a single vowel and a consonant, double the final consonant and add **-ed:** Thunder <u>clapped</u> in the sky.
- When a verb ends in a **consonant** and **y,** change the **y** to **i** before adding **-ed:** We <u>hurried</u> home.
- An **irregular verb** does not end in **-ed** in the past tense: He <u>felt</u> afraid. We <u>grew</u> nervous. Memorize irregular verbs or use a dictionary.

More Irregular Verbs

are/were	feed/fed	is/was	spin/spun
break/broke	get/got	know/knew	sweep/swept
come/came	give/gave	run/ran	think/thought
drink/ drank	hear/heard	say/said	write/wrote

 A Write the correct verb form in ( ) to complete each sentence.

1. A tornado (were, is) a very powerful storm.
2. One tornado (spun, spinned) at more than 300 miles an hour.
3. The National Weather Service (try, tries) to warn people.
4. Hurricanes (cause, causes) a great deal of damage too.
5. Now we (knew, know) what to do in a dangerous storm.

B Write the correct tense to complete the sentences in each column.

Present Tense	Past Tense
1. It rains hard.	It _____ hard.
2. We _____ about hiding.	We thought about hiding.
3. People get wet.	People _____ wet.
4. We run to shelter.	We _____ to shelter.
5. Rabbits hop to their holes.	Rabbits _____ to their holes.
6. Our clothes _____ quickly.	Our clothes dried quickly.
7. Animals drink rainwater.	Animals _____ rainwater.
8. They _____ thirsty.	They were thirsty.
9. Soon it _____ sunny.	Soon it was sunny.
10. We hurry back outside.	We _____ back outside.

C Change the verb in each sentence to the past tense.
Write the new sentences.

11. The tornado moves over the plains.
12. It sweeps across the flat land.
13. Rabbits jump in their holes.
14. Dogs scurry in their yards.
15. The wind rips through the trees.
16. It is the worst tornado in the past ten years.
17. We think about all the necessary repairs.

Review and Assess

Write each sentence using the underlined verb. Use the tense in ( ).

1. Laura <u>run</u> into the barn. (past)
2. She always <u>care</u> for the horses. (present)
3. First, she <u>feed</u> them. (past)
4. Then she <u>give</u> her favorite horse a sugar cube. (past)
5. Laura <u>love</u> working with the horses. (present)

Write the letter of the verb that correctly completes each sentence.

6. After the storm, Jack's dog _____ home.

   A came   **C** comes
   B comed   **D** camed

7. Jack _____ glad to see him.

   A are   **C** be
   B was   **D** were

8. The wind _____ many windows.

   A broken   **C** breaked
   B broked   **D** broke

9. Yesterday neighbors _____ by to repair the damage.

   A droped   **C** dropped
   B drop   **D** dropping

10. Afterwards they _____ it was the worst storm in years.

    A said   **C** saided
    B sayed   **D** say

Replacing Dull Verbs

If you use verbs such as *say, go,* and *get* too often, your writing will sound dull. Try replacing these verbs to improve your style.

- The baby <u>went</u> outside. Whiskers <u>went</u> after her.
  Then Mom <u>went</u> after the baby.
- The baby <u>crawled</u> outside. Whiskers <u>scampered</u> after her.
  Then Mom <u>rushed</u> after the baby.

A Choose a word from the box to replace each underlined word. Use the past-tense form of the new word to write sentences.

> **Words for *say/said***   report, shout, boast
> **Words for *go/went***   scurry, rip, hide, scatter

1. The weatherman <u>said</u> that a tornado had struck Aborine. **2.** It <u>went</u> through the downtown area in twenty minutes. **3.** People <u>went</u> to the public shelter. **4.** City employees with bullhorns <u>said</u> where to go. **5.** Some people <u>went</u> in their basements. **6.** In the wind, things <u>went</u> in all directions. **7.** Later, the mayor <u>said</u> that Aborine had the best tornado recovery plan in the state.

B Replace the underlined word with a past-tense verb of your own.

8. Yesterday we <u>got</u> a report about a tornado. **9.** I <u>got</u> my portable radio from the shelf. **10.** When the power went out, Mom <u>got</u> candles. **11.** Then we <u>got</u> to a safe area downstairs. **12.** I <u>got</u> pictures of the damage.

C Write a short article that compares and contrasts two types of weather.

Review of Verbs

An **action verb** tells what a subject does: The cobra <u>hisses</u> at the mongoose. A **linking verb** tells what a subject is or is like: We <u>are</u> afraid.

All verbs must **agree** with their subjects in a sentence: The cobra <u>rattles</u> its tail. The cobras <u>rattle</u> their tails.

The **tense** of a verb shows the time of the action. A verb in the **present tense** shows action that is happening now: We <u>live</u> in India now. A verb in the **past tense** shows action that has already happened. It often ends in **-ed:** Last year we <u>lived</u> in India. A verb in the **future tense** shows action that will happen: Next year we <u>will live</u> in India.

An **irregular verb** does not follow a pattern: The mongoose <u>fought</u> the cobra. You have to remember its past-tense form. Some irregular verbs are listed on page 80.

 A Write the correct form of the verb in ( ) to complete the sentences.

1. Sandra (live, lives) in India.
2. Yesterday she (sat, sits) in a lush garden.
3. Last night she (read, reads) a book.
4. Her parents often (tell, tells) her stories.
5. Some of the stories (is, are) scary.
6. She (knows, knowed) many facts about animals.
7. Sandra (give, gave) several books to her friends.
8. She (went, will go) to England next year.

B Write the verb in each sentence. Then write **present** if the verb is in the present tense. Write **past** if the verb is in the past tense. Write **future** if the verb is in the future tense.

1. Yesterday I saw a flock of birds.
2. Today one of the birds sang a cheerful song.
3. I cried at the lovely music.
4. I will go back to the garden again later tonight.
5. I will wait for my feathered friends.
6. They pick worms for dinner.
7. They drank from a fountain last night.
8. I watched them in silence.
9. They idly flapped their wings.
10. Tonight I will feed them some seeds.

C Write three sentences of your own using the following verbs in the present tense. Then write each sentence in the past tense and the future tense.

11. live
12. think
13. see

Review and Assess

Replace each underlined verb with a verb in the past tense.
Write the new sentences.

1. The rabbit <u>twitches</u> its whiskers.
2. Three muskrats <u>chase</u> a snake.
3. Hunters <u>catch</u> wild turkeys.
4. Hungry dogs <u>beg</u> for food.
5. Quickly the hawk <u>flies</u> away.

Read the following sentences. Write the letter of the word or words
that complete each sentence.

6. This morning, a snake _____ through the grass.

   A slither   **C** slitherd
   B slithered   **D** will slither

7. He _____ a caterpillar moving slowly.

   A see   **C** seeded
   B saw   **D** seen

8. Now the snake _____ happy because he is very hungry.

   A feel   **C** feels
   B will feels   **D** feeled

9. He knows that soon the caterpillar _____ a good meal.

   A make   **C** made
   B maked   **D** will make

10. Last night, the snake _____ on the rock.

   A sleep   **C** slept
   B sleeped   **D** slep

Using Powerful Verbs in Your Writing

Successful writers use verbs to create pictures for readers. These verbs should agree with their subjects and be written in the correct tense.

- **No:** When my parakeet was angry, she talks and her feathers move.
- **Yes:** When my parakeet is angry, she squawks and her feathers fluff.

> **"WOW" VERBS**
>
> **Think of verbs that tell how animals move. What noises do they make?**

A Choose a verb from the box to complete each sentence. Use the tense in ( ).

pounce	scamper	scurry	slither	dig
shed	swoop	crawl	leap	screech
peck	scratch	gnaw	burrow	

1. A bright green snake _____ along the road. (past)
2. Suddenly, a hawk _____ on the snake. (past)
3. In the meadow, a mouse _____ through the grass. (present)
4. If the mouse isn't careful, another animal _____ on him. (future)
5. Some animals _____ into a hole to escape enemies. (present)

B Complete each sentence in the paragraph with a strong verb from the box above or with your own verb. Use the past tense of all verbs.

6. My brother _____ when he saw my snakes. 7. Four snakes _____ in one tank. 8. They _____ their scaly skin. 9. Two hamsters _____ in another tank. 10. They _____ under wood shavings.

C Write a paragraph that compares and contrasts two animals.

Writing a Comparison/ Contrast Essay

A **test** may ask you to write a comparison/contrast essay. Choose subjects that are alike and different. Use words to show likenesses (*and, also*) and differences (*however, but*). Follow the tips below.

USING DETAILS

Provide details to help readers see and taste the foods you are comparing.

Understand the prompt. Make sure you know what to do. A prompt for a comparison/contrast essay could look like this:

> **Write an essay comparing and contrasting two foods you would find in a school cafeteria.**

Key words and phrases are *essay, comparing and contrasting*, and *foods*.

Find a good topic. Make a list of things that you could compare. Write the qualities of each item you name. Then narrow your list to subjects that can best be compared *and* contrasted.

Organize your ideas. Make a comparison/contrast organizer on scratch paper. Fill in a chart like the one below.

SAME		DIFFERENT	
Food: Peas	**Food:** Carrots	**Food:** Peas	**Food:** Carrots
1. Vegetable	1. Vegetable	1. Soft and sweet	1. Crunchy and bitter
2. Good for you	2. Good for you	2. Round and green	2. Long and orange

Write a good beginning. Write a strong topic sentence that presents your idea and grabs your reader's attention.

Develop and elaborate ideas. Use your comparison/contrast organizer to help you focus your writing. You might begin by describing likenesses between your topics and then move on to differences.

Write a strong ending. Use the ending to sum up your thoughts and make a clear statement about your topic.

Check your work. Share your essay with a classmate to get feedback.

See how the essay below addresses the prompt, has a strong beginning, and stays focused on the topic.

Peas and Carrots

1   How do you feel about peas and carrots? Even if you don't like them, it is interesting to see how they are alike and different. Peas and carrots are similar because they are both vegetables. They are also both good for you.

    Even though peas and carrots do not taste the same, I like to eat them both. Peas are soft and sweet, but carrots are crunchy and slightly bitter. Peas and carrots look different too. Peas are round and green. However, carrots are long and orange. Even though these vegetables are different in some ways, I love to eat them both.

2
3
4
5

1. The first sentence grabs the reader's attention.
2. Words such as *crunchy* and *bitter* appeal to the senses.
3. The writer has a firm command of subject-verb agreement.
4. Key words are used to show a clear contrast.
5. This strong ending sums up the writer's thoughts.

Adjectives

An **adjective** is a word that describes a noun or pronoun.
An adjective usually comes before the word it describes, but it can
also follow it. Many adjectives answer the question *What kind?* These
adjectives describe color, shape, size, sound, taste, touch, or smell.

- **What kind:** The cook put the <u>black</u> pot on the stove.

Other adjectives answer the question *How many?* or *Which one?*
A, an, and *the* are special adjectives called *articles. A* and *an* are used only
with singular nouns. *The* is used with both singular and plural nouns.

- **How many:** She filled <u>six</u> pots with water. Then she lifted <u>a</u> pot.
- **Which one:** <u>This</u> pot is for <u>the</u> soup.

A Write the sentences and underline each adjective.

1. Many authors write stories about animals.
2. These stories sometimes have animals that talk.
3. I love stories about clever animals.
4. Sometimes I read them to my younger sister.

Read each sentence. Write whether the underlined adjective
answers the question **What kind?, How many?,** or **Which one?**

5. The chicken walked by a <u>small</u> stream.
6. <u>Three</u> deer watched the chicken.
7. <u>These</u> deer wanted to meet the chicken.
8. They jumped over a <u>high</u> wall.
9. The <u>friendly</u> chicken greeted the deer.

B Write an adjective from the box to complete each sentence.

one	frightened	dark
four	brave	this

    1. My grandmother told me a story about _____ goats.
2. They lived in a _____ forest by a river. **3.** One day the goats saw a woodcutter fall into _____ river. **4.** _____ goat jumped into the river and swam to the woodcutter. **5.** He told the _____ woodcutter to grab on to his neck. **6.** Then the _____ goat carried the woodcutter to safety.

C Complete each sentence with an adjective of your own. Write the sentences.

   7. The _____ fox chased the chicken.

   8. Then the _____ chicken hid in the barn.

   9. _____ horses looked after the chicken.

  10. These horses guarded a _____ door.

  11. Finally, the fox gave up and returned to the _____ woods.

  12. "I am not a very _____ creature," he moaned.

  13. Instead of chicken, the fox ate a _____ apple.

  14. Maybe tomorrow will be a _____ day for him.

Review and Assess

Each sentence contains two adjectives. One has been underlined.
Write the other adjective.

1. I visited <u>a</u> large farm with my uncle.
2. <u>The</u> farm had two bulls.
3. One bull swished its <u>long</u> tail back and forth.
4. I read about a <u>black</u> bull that used its tail to churn butter.
5. <u>That</u> bull made creamy butter day and night.

Write the letter of the adjective that best completes each sentence.

6. The _____ sun shines on the land.

   A noisy   **C** three
   B hot   **D** that

7. A _____ wind rustles the leaves.

   A one   **C** that
   B hungry   **D** gentle

8. Frogs leap onto the _____ bank of a pond.

   A tired   **C** grassy
   B jumpy   **D** nine

9. Rabbits dig their holes in the _____ ground.

   A four   **C** moist
   B that   **D** under

10. Have you ever seen such a _____ place?

    A much   **C** the
    B mean   **D** peaceful

Using Clear Adjectives in Your Writing

Adjectives can make directions clear for readers.

- Table Tennis is an <u>easy</u> game to play. All you need are <u>two</u> paddles, a ball, and a <u>flat</u> table. The <u>first</u> step is to hit the ball across the table.

A Choose an adjective from the box to complete each sentence. Then write the paragraph.

ten	sharp	empty	one	bigger	old

Ball-Box Toss

1. Find a cardboard box that is _____. **2.** Ask an adult to use a _____ knife to cut a circle in one side. **3.** Make sure the circle is _____ than a tennis ball. **4.** Stand _____ feet from the box. **5.** Toss _____ tennis balls into the hole. **6.** Score _____ point for each ball that goes through the hole into the box.

B Think of a game that you would like to teach somebody. Write the answer to each question below.

7. What do you need to play the game?
8. How many people can play the game at one time?
9. What do you do first to play the game?
10. What are the next steps?
11. How do you win the game?

C Use your answers in Exercise B to write a how-to paragraph. Add an introductory sentence. Use time-order words such as *first* and *then*. Use at least two specific adjectives.

Using Adjectives to Improve Sentences

Adjectives can add clear and descriptive details to sentences. Use only as many adjectives as you need to express your ideas clearly. Too many adjectives can make a sentence confusing.

- **Too little detail:** The pigs lived in a house.
- **Adjectives add detail:** The <u>three</u> pigs lived in a <u>brick</u> house.
- **Too many adjectives:** The three silly, confused, tired little pigs lived in a large and strong brick house.

A Choose the better adjective in ( ) to add a descriptive detail to each sentence. Write the adjective you choose.

1. A (sly, polite) wolf tried to blow the brick house down.
2. Three (frightened, scary) pigs refused to let him in.
3. Then the (sleepy, hungry) wolf licked his lips.
4. "I will try to fool the pigs," the (sneaky, kind) wolf said.
5. However, the wolf could not fool the (bored, three) pigs.
6. Do you think that he had a (tiny, clever) plan?
7. I thought this was an (eager, interesting) story.

The following sentences have too many adjectives. Choose one of the underlined adjectives in each sentence. Rewrite each sentence, using the adjective you have chosen.

8. The <u>smart, intelligent, thoughtful</u> jury found the wolf guilty.
9. Of course, the <u>angry, nervous, upset</u> wolf said he was not guilty.
10. Now the wolf and the pigs are <u>close, wonderful, best</u> friends.

B Add an adjective to improve each sentence.
Write the new sentences.

1. The _____ pigs laughed at the wolf.
2. They told the _____ wolf that he would never win.
3. Then the wolf vowed to blow down the pigs' _____ house.
4. Inside the house the pigs opened a _____ window.
5. Suddenly, they felt a _____ gust of wind.

C Write three adjectives you might use to describe each person, place, or thing.

6. Your school: _____ _____ _____
7. Your town: _____ _____ _____
8. Your favorite story: _____ _____ _____
9. Your best friend: _____ _____ _____
10. Your favorite food: _____ _____ _____
11. Your favorite outfit: _____ _____ _____
12. Your room: _____ _____ _____
13. Your neighborhood: _____ _____ _____
14. An apple: _____ _____ _____

Review and Assess

Add an adjective to improve each sentence. Write the new sentences.

1. The birds sang a song.
2. All the animals had a party.
3. They danced together and ate pies.
4. They told stories to one another.
5. One story was about pigs and a wolf.

Read the following paragraph. Write the letter of the adjective that adds a descriptive detail to each sentence.

   6. Penny was a _____ dog. **7.** In the summer she liked to chase _____ butterflies. **8.** One day as she was about to catch one, it turned to her and said, "If you spare me, I'll show you a _____ stream." **9.** Penny agreed and spent the rest of the summer splashing and playing with the _____ animals by the stream. **10.** In the fall the _____ dog looked for the butterfly to thank it.

6. A one   **C** hard
   B that   **D** playful

7. A this   **C** empty
   B orange   **D** one

8. A refreshing   **C** brave
   B funny   **D** crazy

9. A shut   **C** friendly
   B twinkling   **D** those

10. A open   **C** light
   B grateful   **D** these

Using Adjectives to Improve Sentences

Use specific adjectives to paint clear pictures in a how-to report.

- I am <u>careful</u> when I wash my dog. First, I wet her <u>dirty</u> fur.
Then I add <u>generous</u> amounts of shampoo. When she is <u>clean</u>,
I rinse and dry her well. I give her <u>tasty</u> biscuits when I am done.

A Replace each underlined adjective with an adjective from the box.

scrubbed	three	fresh	colorful
entertaining	constant	graceful	

1. I have spent many <u>neat</u> moments watching my goldfish.
2. They move like <u>good</u> ballet dancers. **3.** Goldfish do not require <u>much</u>
care. **4.** First, fill their bowl with <u>good</u> water. **5.** Then put <u>pretty</u> stones
in their bowls. **6.** Give them <u>some</u> shakes from the food box every day.
7. Make sure their bowls are always <u>nice</u>.

B Complete each sentence in the paragraph with a strong adjective
of your own. Write the new paragraph.

8. I read about a girl who taught her parrot _____ tricks. **9.** She
taught him how to answer a _____ telephone. **10.** She repeated the
_____ command to "Answer it." **11.** After _____ hours, the parrot
could use its beak to push the answer button when the phone rang.
12. Then he said "Hello" in a _____ voice.

C Work with a group to write directions for playing tick-tack-toe. Use
some of these adjectives to describe the lines you must draw to enclose
the Xs and Os: *horizontal, vertical, parallel, straight.*

Comparative and Superlative Adjectives

Adjectives can be used to compare people, places, things, or groups.

A **comparative** adjective compares two items. Add **-er** to most adjectives to make them comparative: **taller.** Use **more** with long adjectives such as **incredible** to make them comparative: **more incredible.**

A **superlative** adjective compares three or more items. Add **-est** to the end of most adjectives to make them superlative: **greatest.** Use **most** with long adjectives such as **fantastic** to make them superlative: **most fantastic.**

- For most adjectives that end with a consonant and **y**, change the **y** to **i** before adding **-er** or **-est: silly, sillier, silliest.**
- For most adjectives that end in a single consonant after a single vowel, double the final consonant before adding **-er** or **-est: hot, hotter, hottest.**
- If an adjective ends with **e,** drop the final **e** before adding **-er** or **-est: tame, tamer, tamest.**
- Adjectives such as **good** and **bad** have **irregular** comparative and superlative forms: **good, better, best; bad, worse, worst.**

A Write the comparative and superlative form of each adjective.

1.–8. neat, fine, high, ugly, shiny, tan, beautiful, exciting

B Choose the correct form of the adjective in ( ) to complete each sentence. Write the sentences.

1. Jay uses a (heavy) bat than Aaron does.
2. Is Jay the (strong) player on the team?
3. Of all the players, Vera is the (fast) runner.
4. She is even a (good) fielder than Jay.
5. In fact, she is the (talented) fielder on the team.
6. Is baseball a (enjoyable) sport than golf?
7. I consider golf the (dull) sport in the world!
8. Dad thinks that golf is the (exciting) sport of all.
9. He says the (hard) thing to do is to hit a golf ball.

C Change the underlined adjective to the kind of adjective in ( ). Write the new sentence.

10. My tennis racket is <u>light</u> than yours. (comparative)
11. Our <u>fine</u> skater sprained his ankle. (superlative)
12. Nira is a <u>good</u> soccer player than I am. (comparative)
13. Sam has the <u>good</u> fastball on the team. (superlative)
14. Soccer is the <u>popular</u> sport at school. (superlative)
15. Is our pool <u>big</u> than yours? (comparative)
16. The Links have the <u>bad</u> record in the league. (superlative)

Review and Assess

Complete each sentence by writing the correct form of the underlined adjective.

1. Eddy is the <u>swift</u> runner in school.
2. He is the <u>new</u> member of the track team.
3. He has <u>good</u> times than anyone else on the team.
4. When we run together, he takes <u>long</u> strides than I do.
5. Certainly, he is the <u>fantastic</u> runner I have ever seen.

Write the letter of the word or words that complete each sentence.

6. A soccer ball is _____than a football.

   A rounder   **C** more round
   B roundest   **D** most round

7. Many people claim that running is the _____ sport to learn.

   A easy   **C** easier
   B easiest   **D** most easy

8. Some people believe that lacrosse is the _____ sport of all.

   A difficult   **C** more difficult
   B less difficult   **D** most difficult

9. In my opinion, tennis is a _____ game than football.

   A safe   **C** safest
   B safer   **D** most safe

10. Did you know that a hockey puck is _____ than a baseball?

    A heavy   **C** heavier
    B heaviest   **D** heavyer

Making Comparisons in Your Writing

Writers use different forms of adjectives to help readers understand what they are explaining. Comparative and superlative adjectives can tell the reader exactly what to do.

- Choose the <u>shortest</u> bat that is comfortable for you. With a <u>lighter</u> bat you can swing fast. In general, the <u>most talented</u> hitters use the bat that is <u>best</u> for them.

A Write each sentence using the correct form of the adjective in ( ). Then add two more sentences, using comparative and superlative adjectives.

1. Hitting a baseball is (easy) than you think. **2.** Keep your head still, the way the (successful) hitters in the major leagues do. **3.** Use a (loose) grip than you think you might need. **4.** Now your (great) challenge will be to keep your eye on the ball. **5.** With practice, you may become a (good) hitter than you ever thought you could be.

B Write an opening sentence and a closing sentence for this how-to paragraph. Use comparative or superlative adjectives to make your sentences clear. Write the new paragraph.

First, keep your eye on the quarterback. Then follow the twirling ball as it comes toward you. Hold out both hands as it gets closer. Once you catch the football, tuck it under one arm. Hold it tightly and run toward the goal post.

C Write a paragraph telling how to play your favorite sport. Include comparative and superlative adjectives.

Adverbs

An **adverb** is a word that tells how, when, or where something happens. Most adverbs tell about verbs. An adverb can appear before or after a verb. Many adverbs that tell *how* something is done end in **-ly.**

- **How:** Anna <u>eagerly</u> reads books. She loves reading <u>quietly</u>.
- **When:** <u>Yesterday</u> she read. She <u>always</u> reads on Sunday.
- **Where:** Anna sits <u>outside</u> and writes in her journal.

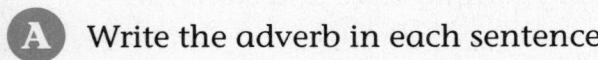 **A** Write the adverb in each sentence.

1. Alicia walked slowly to school. **2.** She carefully crossed the busy streets. **3.** Alicia often takes the same route to school. **4.** Sometimes she meets a friend along the way. **5.** They wait outside until the school bell rings.

Read each sentence. Write **how** if the underlined adverb tells how an action happens. Write **when** if the underlined adverb tells when an action happens. Write **where** if the underlined adverb tells where an action happens.

6. Mai's school day <u>always</u> begins with Chinese lessons.
7. Students chat <u>quietly</u> until the teacher arrives.
8. Then Mai and the students <u>politely</u> greet the teacher.
9. The teacher looks <u>around</u> to see if all students are present.
10. Mai <u>eagerly</u> studies the Chinese language.
11. <u>Tomorrow</u> the class will study Chinese calligraphy.
12. The characters that form words must be drawn <u>carefully</u>.

B Write the adverb in each sentence. Write **how** if the adverb tells how something happens. Write **when** if the adverb tells when something happens. Write **where** if the adverb tells where something happens.

1. Julie often plays with her friends.
2. They run around and play games.
3. Sometimes they play hide-and-seek.
4. Julie covers her eyes and slowly counts to ten.
5. All of her friends run wildly and hide.
6. Soon Julie is searching for her friends.
7. She looks everywhere.
8. Finally, she finds the last person.
9. It rarely takes her over five minutes.
10. Tomorrow they will play a different game.

C Write five sentences of your own using the verbs and adverbs in the box.

Verbs		Adverbs	
speak	aim	upwards	rarely
read	fall	carefully	often
drive		softly	

Review and Assess

Write the adverb in each sentence.

1. Don will never forget visiting Korea with his mother.
2. His mother was born there.
3. Recently, Don and his mother visited Korean relatives.
4. Don's grandparents warmly welcomed him.
5. Don frequently writes to his relatives.

Write the letter of the correct answer to each question.

6. Which word is an adverb that tells how something happened?

   A behind   **C** soon

   B never   **D** slowly

7. Which word is an adverb that tells when something happened?

   A instantly   **C** only

   B over   **D** openly

8. Which word is an adverb that tells where something happened?

   A freely   **C** fully

   B there   **D** bed

9. Which word is an adverb?

   A quietly   **C** quit

   B queen   **D** quiz

10. Which word is not an adverb?

    A upward   **C** noisily

    B hills   **D** yesterday

Using Adverbs to Show Time Order

Use adverbs to show the order of steps in a how-to report.

- To make a kite, <u>first</u> gather materials such as paper, balsa wood, scissors, glue, cloth, and string. <u>Then</u> think of a design and draw it on the paper. <u>Now</u> cut out the design and attach the paper to a frame made out of balsa wood. <u>Finally,</u> attach the cloth tail and string.

A Put the sentences in the correct order. Add one of these adverbs to each sentence to show the order of steps: *Third, Finally, First, Now, Second.* Write the how-to paragraph.

1. _____ make a head out of clay.
2. I just learned how to make a finger puppet. _____ I will show you how.
3. _____ gather your materials.
4. _____ place the finished head over your finger and have fun!
5. _____ paint the head and wait for it to dry.

B Put the sentences for this explanation of how to make a walkie-talkie in order. Then add adverbs such as *first* and *finally* to show time order. Add an opening and a closing sentence. Write the finished report.

6. Connect the cans with the string and tie a knot at each end.
7. Take two clean, empty cans and about ten feet of string. 8. Have two people stand apart from each other so that the string is taut.
9. Poke a hole through the bottom of each can.

C Explain how to make a sandwich or snack. Use adverbs to make the order of steps clear.

Using Adverbs to Improve Sentences

....

Use adverbs to add descriptive details to your sentences. Use only as many adverbs as you need. Too many adverbs can make a sentence confusing.

....

- **Original sentence:** My grandmother celebrated her birthday.
- **Adverb adds detail:** My grandmother <u>quietly</u> celebrated her birthday.
- **Too much detail:** My grandmother <u>quietly, calmly, peacefully</u> celebrated her birthday.

A Write the adverb in each sentence.

1. Yesterday, Matt looked for a birthday present for his mom.
2. His dad kindly offered to drive him to the mall.
3. Matt was sure he would find the perfect gift there.
4. He patiently looked but could not find a thing.
5. Finally, Matt decided to make his mother a present.

Choose an adverb from the box to add a descriptive detail to each sentence. Write the new paragraph.

outside	never	closely	always	quickly

6. On breezy summer evenings, Grandma liked to sit _____.
7. She _____ told stories. 8. I listened _____ to every word. 9. She spoke _____ when she told an exciting story. 10. Grandma _____ forgot a single detail.

B Each sentence below has too many details. Choose one adverb from each sentence. Rewrite the sentence, using only that adverb.

1. Terry really, truly, deeply loves playing baseball.
2. He constantly practices hitting always daily.
3. Terry frequently goes to Wrigley Field often.
4. He loudly, happily, noisily cheers for the Cubs.
5. Terry especially, particularly, mainly enjoys sitting in the bleachers.
6. Once yesterday he even caught a fly ball.
7. Terry is happy because he never rarely sees the Cubs lose.

C Write an adverb of your own to complete each sentence.

8. Eric's mother told stories _____.
9. She _____ explained the importance of traditions.
10. Eric _____ liked listening to stories about Africa.
11. _____, his mother told about a mongoose and a bear.
12. The bear _____ chased the poor mongoose.
13. How _____ that bear growled!
14. _____ the bear caught the mongoose.
15. They became friends and lived together _____.

Review and Assess

Choose an adverb from the box to add descriptive detail to each sentence. Write the new sentences.

> downstairs carefully quietly never immediately

1. Greg _____ wrapped his handmade book.
2. Then he ran _____ and placed the gift on Ana's chair.
3. Ana said she had _____ received such a wonderful present.
4. She raced to a tree in the backyard and _____ sat down.
5. The backyard was peaceful, as Ana _____ read her book.

Read each sentence. Write the letter of the word that is an adverb.

6. Jenny eagerly counted the minutes until her birthday party.

   A until   **C** eagerly
   B counted   **D** birthday

7. She glanced nervously at the clock as she waited for her guests to arrive.

   A glanced   **C** nervously
   B at   **D** as

8. Suddenly, the doorbell rang and Jenny heard familiar voices.

   A Suddenly   **C** rang
   B doorbell   **D** familiar

9. One of her friends generously gave her a DVD as a gift.

   A her   **C** generously
   B friends   **D** gave

Using Adverbs to Improve Sentences

You have learned that adverbs show *when* to do each step of a how-to report. Adverbs also tell *how* to do these steps.

- Cut the cover for your scrapbook <u>carefully</u> out of construction paper. Glue pictures <u>securely</u> on the cover.

A Choose an adverb from the box to add to each sentence in the explanation. Write the new paragraph.

closely	fast	generously	gently	exactly

1. Cooking pasta is easy, if you _____ follow directions. **2.** First, add the pasta to _____ boiling water. **3.** Then cook _____ as long as the directions say. **4.** Now strain the pasta _____ so it doesn't get cold. **5.** Toss pasta with butter or your favorite sauce and sprinkle _____ with cheese.

B Use adverbs of your own to make each sentence in this how-to report clear.

6. A homemade scrapbook is something you will treasure _____. **7.** You can _____ put one together in an afternoon. **8.** Glue artwork, photographs, and mementos, such as ticket stubs and letters, _____ to the pages so that nothing comes loose. **9.** _____ write a title on the cover. **10.** _____ show your scrapbook to friends and family.

C Write a how-to report about something you do regularly, such as brushing your teeth, making breakfast, or operating a DVD player. Use adverbs that tell *how* in your report.

Writing a How-to Report

A **test** may ask you to explain how to do something. Include all the steps. Use words such as *first* and *finally* show the order of steps. Follow the tips below.

VISUALIZE
Picture the steps in your mind.

Understand the prompt. Make sure you know what to do. Read the prompt carefully. A prompt for a how-to explanation could look like this:

> **Write a report that gives steps on how to make or do something. Make your report interesting to read and easy to understand. Explain all the steps and materials needed.**

Key words and phrases are *report*, *how to*, and *steps and materials*.

Find a good topic. Think of things that you have done before. Choose a topic that you can explain in a few simple steps.

Organize your ideas. Make a how-to chart on scratch paper. Your chart might look like this:

TASK	STEPS
Searching the Internet	1. Turn on computer.
	2. Connect to the Internet.
	3. Find a search engine.
	4. Type in words about your topic.
	5. Narrow your search.

Write a good beginning. Write a strong topic sentence.

Develop and elaborate ideas. Use your chart to help focus your writing. Include words such as *first* and *then* to show order.

Write a strong ending. Sum up your thoughts and provide a clear closing.

Check your work. Share your work with a classmate to get ideas and suggestions on how to improve your report.

See how the report below addresses the prompt, has a strong beginning and end, and stays focused on the topic.

Searching the Internet

Have you ever needed to find information quickly? —— 1
The Internet is a great way to get facts fast. You'll need a
computer with access to the Internet. Use a modem or even DSL,
which is a type of high-speed connection to the Internet.

4 —
Of course, the first thing you do is turn on the computer.
Then connect it to the Internet and log on to a search engine,
such as Google. Now, type a word or words about your topic — 2
3 — into the search box. Specific words can help narrow your
search. If you type a general word, such as <u>dog</u>, you will get
a million responses. Finally, visit links the search engine gives
you. Now you have information at your fingertips. —— 5

---

1. This question grabs the reader's attention.
2. The writer uses words that show the order of steps.
3. Strong adjectives make the information clear.
4. Special terms are defined.
5. This strong ending sums up the writer's purpose.

Pronouns

Pronouns are words that replace nouns or noun phrases. *I, you, he, she, it, me, him,* and *her* are singular pronouns. *We, you, they, us,* and *them* are plural pronouns. The singular pronoun *I* is always capitalized.

- <u>Susan</u> started <u>the car,</u> and <u>Jenny and Pam</u> hopped in.
- <u>She</u> parked <u>it</u> at the restaurant, and <u>they</u> went inside.

Possessive Pronouns show who or what owns something and take the place of possessive nouns. *My, your, his, her,* and *its* are singular possessive pronouns. *Our, your,* and *their* are plural possessive pronouns. Possessive pronouns do not have an apostrophe.

- Is that <u>Dawn's</u> new car? It looks like <u>the Smiths'</u> car.
- Is that <u>her</u> new car? It looks like <u>their</u> car.

 Write the pronoun in each sentence.

1. Every summer my family takes a long car trip.
2. Next year we are going to San Antonio.
3. Last year I went to the Grand Canyon.
4. Could Nick tell us all about those amazing rocks?
5. A tour guide answered our questions.

Choose a pronoun in ( ) to replace each underlined noun or noun phrase. Write the pronouns you choose.

6. <u>The family</u> drove through the Rocky Mountains. (We, She)
7. <u>Sally</u> and I rode in the back seat. (Her, She)
8. <u>The family's</u> car struggled up the steep roads. (It, Our)
9. <u>Mom and Dad</u> were stunned by the scenery. (Them, They)
10. <u>Dad</u> said, "Let's come back next year." (He, You)

B Replace each underlined noun or noun phrase with a pronoun from the box. One word will be used twice. Write the new sentences.

they	him	it	them

1. <u>George and Brenda</u> got ready to go on a car trip.
2. The tank was empty, so Brenda filled <u>the tank</u> with gas.
3. "Check the tires, George," Brenda warned <u>George.</u>
4. George thought <u>the tires</u> were a little low.
5. After filling <u>the tires,</u> the couple was off!

C Think of a pronoun to complete each sentence. Then write the paragraph.

6. "_____ want to buy a new car," said Frank. 7. "Safety is important to _____," he added. 8. "What do _____ recommend?" Frank asked Tim Aldi, the car dealer. 9. _____ told Frank to get side airbags. 10. Then _____ asked the dealer about antilock brakes. 11. "Let _____ show you a car with these features—and more," said the dealer. 12. "_____ car will be fantastic and safe too!" Frank said proudly. 13. _____ drove the car out of the showroom.

Review and Assess

Write a pronoun to replace each underlined word or words.

1. <u>Ricardo</u> loves maps.
2. "<u>Maps</u> are full of interesting information!" he exclaimed.
3. One day Ricardo saw <u>Anita and Damon</u> reading a map.
4. Ricardo asked if he could look at <u>Anita's</u> map.
5. <u>Anita, Damon, and Ricardo</u> studied the map together.

Read the following paragraph. Write the letter of the word that completes each sentence.

6. Last year _____ went on a trip across the country with our dog.
7. _____ is a wonderful dog! **8.** Three of _____ friends were visiting Yellowstone National Park when we were there. **9.** _____ saw Old Faithful.
10. The park ranger told the tourists, "_____ can take pictures, but do not get too close." **11.** The ranger warned, "If you see bears, do not disturb _____."

6. A it	**9. A** His	
B him	**B** They	
C me	**C** Them	
D we	**D** Their	
7. A He	**10. A** Your	
B His	**B** You	
C They	**C** Me	
D I	**D** Them	
8. A it	**11. A** it	
B him	**B** they	
C my	**C** them	
D you	**D** us	

Using Pronouns to Improve Your Style

Pay attention to your writing style in a research report. Use pronouns to make your sentences smoother and less wordy. Avoid beginning too many sentences with the same pronoun.

- Why are gasless cars special? <u>Gasless cars</u> cause less pollution.
- Why are gasless cars special? <u>They</u> cause less pollution.

A Use pronouns to replace the underlined nouns or noun phrases.

1. Today most cars pollute the air because <u>these cars</u> use gasoline. **2.** Years ago, scientists only dreamed of gasless cars, but today people actually drive <u>these cars.</u> **3.** Hydrogen is used in some cars because <u>hydrogen</u> is a gas that burns cleanly. **4.** My aunt is a scientist, and <u>my aunt</u> feels that gas-powered cars will disappear in the next 50 years.

B Edit this paragraph to make the style smoother. Add pronouns in the spaces shown. Then rearrange or replace words so that sentences 6–9 do not all begin with *They*. Write the new paragraph.

5. Many people own cars because _____ need to get to places quickly. **6.** They might also walk to school or work because it is important for _____ to get exercise. **7.** They tell us that 30 minutes of exercise a day can improve _____ health. **8.** They say that walking helps our hearts and keeps _____ beating regularly. **9.** They are learning that cars may be necessary, but _____ aren't as good for your health as walking.

C Write a paragraph about the transportation you use. Don't forget your bike and your feet.

Subject and Object Pronouns

A **subject pronoun** is used in the subject of a sentence. Singular subject pronouns are *I, you, he, she,* and *it.* Plural subject pronouns are *we, you,* and *they:* I remember the day. <u>We</u> came to America on a boat.

An **object pronoun** is used in the predicate of a sentence after an action verb or with a preposition, such as *for, at, into,* or *to.* Singular object pronouns are *me, you, him, her,* and *it.* Plural object pronouns are *us, you,* and *them:* The people were very kind to <u>me</u>. They gave <u>us</u> sandwiches.

A **contraction** is a shortened form of two words. An apostrophe takes the place of one or more letters. Contractions can be formed from a pronoun and a verb. Some common contractions are *she'll* (she will), *he'd* (he would *or* he had), *it's* (it is), *I'm* (I am), *we're* (we are), and *they've* (they have).

A Write each subject pronoun or contraction.

1. She'd come to America in 1973.
2. At first, it was a very strange place to her.
3. Then we helped her find a job.
4. After a few days, they found work for her.
5. You'll also have to work hard to get ahead.

Write each object pronoun.

6. Leila, a newcomer to America, seemed shy to us.
7. Imagine how odd the clothes in America looked to her!
8. She asked me for some advice about dressing.
9. "Notice how people dress and copy them," I said.
10. "In time, everything will be easier for you," I added.

B Choose the correct pronoun or pronoun contraction in ( ) to complete each sentence. Write the words you choose.

1. (I, Me) like working with Barry at the store.
2. The customers are friendly, and we like (them, they).
3. Sometimes (they're, they've) a little difficult, though.
4. "Get me a bolt of cloth," one man demanded of (they, me).
5. The boss tells (us, we), "The customer is always right."
6. "No matter how a customer treats (you, she)," he says, "always smile."
7. "May I have a raise?" Barry always asks (he, him).
8. The boss just shrugs and says, "I'll think about (they, it)."
9. "(They, He'll) give me a raise some day," Barry sighs.

C Add a pronoun or pronoun contraction to complete each sentence. Then write the new paragraph.

10. When Carla moved into her new apartment, _____ was excited. 11. She wanted to make _____ a beautiful place. 12. She asked her father if _____ help her fix up the apartment. 13. Together, _____ painted every room a different color. 14. Her father was very helpful, and she thanked _____ many times. 15. He was proud of _____. 16. When Carla is finished moving in, _____ have a party and invite all of her friends. 17. She can't wait for _____ to see her new home.

Review and Assess

Write each sentence. Draw one line under each subject pronoun.
Draw two lines under each object pronoun.

1. Grandmother's friends once threw a surprise party for her.
2. "Don't tell Tina about it!" Grandmother's friends warned.
3. They planned the party for five o'clock.
4. "Will Val bring a card for us to sign?" Shira asked.
5. They had the party in a new restaurant in town.
6. Grandmother loved every minute of it.

Read the following paragraph. Write the letter of the word that
completes each sentence.

7. The first time I saw America, I could hardly believe how beautiful
_____ was. 8. The other passengers were amazed too, and _____ cheered
loudly. 9. When the boat arrived in port, _____ looked over the rail to find
my sister. 10. Finally, I saw her waving to _____. 11. I rushed to meet
_____, and then we gave each other a big hug.

7. **A** you
   B it
   C they
   D he

8. **A** us
   B you
   C them
   D they

9. **A** I
   B her
   C me
   D us

10. **A** I
    B she
    C me
    D they

11. **A** she
    B her
    C you
    D him

Using Subject and Object Pronouns

Pronouns can make your research report clear, but only if you use them correctly. Take care to use the correct forms of pronouns.

- Immigrants who come to the United States speak many languages. Some of <u>they</u> speak Italian, Chinese, and Arabic. (Incorrect)
- Some of <u>them</u> speak Italian, Chinese, and Arabic. (Correct)

A Complete each sentence with a pronoun from the box.

him	they	me	I	it	you	he

1. I will tell _____ about my neighbor, Lin. **2.** _____ immigrated to the United States from China. **3.** His parents brought _____ when he was six. **4.** _____ all spoke only Chinese. **5.** Lin quickly learned English, and now he speaks _____ very well. **6.** Lin told _____ about the history of China. **7.** He asked me if _____ would like to travel there some day with him.

B Write about a place that you have visited or imagine a place that you would like to visit. Complete each sentence with a pronoun and a word or words of your own.

8. (subject pronoun) visited _____ with my family. **9.** (subject pronoun) went there in _____. **10.** (subject pronoun) was exciting because _____. **11.** My family brought many _____ home with (object pronoun). **12.** Some day we will take (object pronoun) with us _____.

C Interview someone who immigrated to the United States. Write about that person's first impressions. Use pronouns correctly.

Pronouns and Referents

A **pronoun** takes the place of a noun. The noun or noun phrase that a pronoun replaces (or *refers* to) is called its **referent**, or **antecedent**. A pronoun and its referent must agree.

- The <u>snow</u> is white, and <u>it</u> blankets the land.

       referent   pronoun

- <u>David and Mel</u> were explorers. <u>They</u> discovered exciting places.

A   Write the correct pronoun in ( ) to complete each sentence. The referents of the pronouns have been underlined to help you.

1. Although <u>Antarctica</u> is a frozen wilderness, (it, his) still has plant and animal life.
2. <u>Explorers</u> were surprised when (him, they) found life there.
3. Our <u>teacher</u> told us that (they, she) had visited Alaska.
4. <u>She and her friend</u> showed us photographs that (them, they) had taken.
5. <u>Alaska</u> is beautiful, and I hope to visit (it, him) some day.

Match the pronoun with the noun or noun phrase that could be its referent. Write the pronoun and its referent.

6. it   **a**   Arctic explorers
7. we   **b**   Arnie
8. he   **c**   Peggy and I
9. they   **d**   Mary
10. she   **e**   ice

B Write a pronoun to replace each underlined noun or noun phrase. The referent may be in the same sentence or in an earlier sentence.

1. Hal followed footprints in the snow as <u>Hal</u> trudged along.
2. <u>These footprints</u> led to a house.
3. <u>The house</u> had smoke pouring out of the chimney.
4. He knocked on the door, and <u>the door</u> was opened immediately.
5. Hal removed his snowshoes and left <u>the snowshoes</u> outside.
6. "Come in," an old man said, as <u>the old man</u> stood aside.
7. Hal sat by the fire and warmed his hands over <u>the fire</u>.
8. The old man brought <u>Hal</u> a cup of soup and some bread.
9. "It's good to see you, Dad," said Hal as <u>Hal</u> began to relax.
10. After both men had talked, <u>both men</u> went to bed.

C Write one or two sentences using each noun and pronoun pair given. Use each noun as the referent of the pronoun next to it.

11. snow, it
12. seals, they
13. explorer, she
14. sled, it
15. boy, him
16. my friend and I, we
17. compass, it

Review and Assess

Write the pronoun in each sentence that agrees with the underlined referent.

1. The glaciers were tall, and they glistened in the sun.
2. As the sun began to set, it cast shadows on the ice.
3. When my brother and I felt tired, we headed home.
4. Our parents waved when they saw my brother's red parka.
5. Mom told my brother and me that she was happy to see us.

Read the following paragraph. Write the letter of the pronoun that correctly completes each sentence. The referents of the pronouns have been underlined.

6. Our team of dogs pulled the sled as _____ sped across the snow.
7. My sister and I were happy when _____ saw the igloo. 8. The dogs were so hungry that _____ gobbled up their food. 9. Ernest was my favorite dog because _____ always slept at my side. 10. Ernest curled up beside his sister, Ernestine, to keep _____ warm.

6. **A** it   **C** them
   B he   **D** her

7. **A** us   **C** we
   B it   **D** her

8. **A** it   **C** them
   B they   **D** her

9. **A** her   **C** he
   B we   **D** I

10. **A** her   **C** his
    B she   **D** us

Using Pronouns in Your Writing

Choose words carefully in your research report. Use pronouns correctly to make your writing clear and smooth.

A Change the underlined nouns or noun phrases to pronouns. Write the new paragraph.

1. Robert Peary kept trying to reach the North Pole. <u>Peary</u> made his first attempt in 1893. **2.** Like all Arctic explorers, Peary fought freezing temperatures. <u>All Arctic explorers</u> also fought heavy winds. **3.** Peary failed to reach the Pole in 1893, but <u>Peary</u> did not give up. **4.** In 1908, Peary, Matt Henson, and four Inuit explorers set out to reach the North Pole. <u>These six explorers</u> thought they had reached the North Pole on April 6, 1909. **5.** Later, experts examined Peary's diary. <u>The diary</u> showed that they may have missed the Pole because of errors in navigation.

B Write a pronoun to complete each sentence. Then write two sentences of your own about space exploration.

6. Astronauts are explorers in space. _____ study space by doing experiments. **7.** Alan Shepard was the first American in space. _____ went in 1961. **8.** Neil Armstrong and Buzz Aldrin were the first men to land on the moon. _____ landed in 1969. **9.** The moon landing was exciting because _____ was a "first." **10.** Sally Ride was the first American woman to travel into space. _____ made her historic flight in 1983.

C Write a paragraph about a person or group who did something special. Use pronouns to make your writing smooth.

Prepositions and Prepositional Phrases

A **preposition** is a word that shows how a noun or a pronoun is related to other words in the same sentence. A preposition begins a group of words called a **prepositional phrase.** At the end of the phrase is a noun or a pronoun called the **object of the preposition.** A prepositional phrase can be used to tell *where, when, how,* or *which one.*

- **Preposition:** The turtle buried its eggs <u>in</u> the sand.
- **Prepositional phrase:** <u>in the sand</u>
- **Object of the preposition:** <u>sand</u>

<table>
<tr><td colspan="5" align="center">**Common Prepositions**</td></tr>
<tr><td>about</td><td>around</td><td>between</td><td>into</td><td>to</td></tr>
<tr><td>above</td><td>at</td><td>by</td><td>of</td><td>under</td></tr>
<tr><td>across</td><td>behind</td><td>for</td><td>on</td><td>upon</td></tr>
<tr><td>after</td><td>below</td><td>from</td><td>over</td><td>with</td></tr>
<tr><td>along</td><td>beneath</td><td>in</td><td>through</td><td>without</td></tr>
</table>

 Write each sentence. Underline the prepositional phrase. Then circle the object of the preposition.

1. Crabs scoot behind a rock.
2. Tropical fish swim in schools.
3. Along the sandy bottom crawls a snail.
4. Is that an octopus darting through the water?
5. Many creatures live beneath the waves.

B Each sentence below contains two prepositional phrases.
Write the prepositional phrases.

1. Sea turtles face many dangers on land and in the sea.
2. Turtles at sea can die in fishing nets.
3. Eggs in a beach nest may be destroyed by other animals.
4. People in cars drive over beach nests and crush the eggs.
5. Birds with sharp beaks catch baby turtles on the sand.
6. The bright lights of beach resorts may confuse baby turtles as they head for the sea.
7. People around the world protect sea turtles from danger.

C Add a prepositional phrase of your own to each sentence.
Write the new sentences.

8. Many kinds of fish live _____.
9. Tito likes to collect shells _____.
10. Clumps of seaweed float _____.
11. Waves crash loudly _____.
12. The setting sun cast a glow _____.
13. Do all turtles live _____?
14. Sea turtles build their nests _____.
15. Can turtles survive _____?
16. Turtles are not always safe _____.

Review and Assess

Write each sentence. Put one line under the prepositional phrase.
Put two lines under the object of the preposition.

1. The young dog ran along the beach.
2. She barked at the gulls.
3. The gulls calmly floated on the water.
4. They ignored the dog with the loud bark.
5. Soon the dog grew bored and ran through the grass.

Write the letter of the preposition that completes each sentence.

6. Some fish swim _____ other fish to find food.

   A because   **C** with
   B of   **D** none

7. A fish may find food _____ the surface of the water.

   A near   **C** of
   B without   **D** after

8. Other fish search for food _____ a reef.

   A since   **C** happily
   B around   **D** to

9. Seals like to lie _____ rocks in the sun.

   A on   **C** warm
   B after   **D** swim

10. When the seals get hot, they dive _____ the sea.

    A gentle   **C** above
    B listen   **D** into

Using Prepositional Phrases to Add Details

Use prepositional phrases to provide information in your research report.

- Sea turtles dig nests <u>in the moist sand</u>.

A Improve the paragraph below by adding a prepositional phrase from the box to each sentence. Write the new sentences.

into the air	in the sea	in one gulp
around the world	to only a few countries	

1. Whales are the largest animals _____. **2.** They can swallow hundreds of fish _____. **3.** When whales surface, they often blow huge streams of water _____. **4.** People used to hunt for whales all _____. **5.** Now whale hunting is limited _____.

B Think of an animal you know something about. Then write answers to the questions below.

   6. Which animal are you describing?
   7. What does your animal look like?
   8. How does your animal change from baby to adult?
   9. How does your animal move?
10. Where does your animal live?
11. What does your animal eat?
12. What are your animal's natural enemies?

C Use your answers to **6.–12.** to help you write a short article about your animal. Use prepositional phrases to give information.

Conjunctions

Conjunctions are connecting words, such as *and, or,* and *but.* Conjunctions can be used to join words, phrases, and sentences. They also make compound subjects, compound predicates, and compound sentences.

Compound subject: <u>Mars and Venus</u> are planets.

Compound predicate: The *Magellan* spacecraft <u>landed on Venus and took pictures</u>.

Compound sentence: Mars is a planet, but the sun is a star. (Note the comma.)

- Use *and* to join related ideas: Pluto is small and icy.
- Use *but* to join different ideas: Saturn has rings, but the moon has craters.
- Use *or* to suggest a choice: All the planets are very hot or very cold.

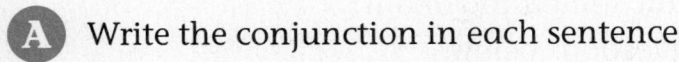 **A** Write the conjunction in each sentence.

1. Jupiter is the largest planet, and it spins very fast.
2. Saturn's rings are made of ice and icy rock.
3. There may have been life on Mars, but we are not sure.
4. One day I will go to another planet or the moon.
5. Mars has two moons, but it does not have any rings.
6. Saturn and Jupiter are the largest planets in the solar system.
7. Saturn is large, but Jupiter is larger.
8. A planet or other huge object may have knocked Uranus on its side.
9. Computers and telescopes help us study planets.

B Use the conjunction *and, or,* or *but* to join each pair of sentences. Write the new sentences. Remember to add a comma.

1. Would you like to visit Mars? Would you rather go to Venus?
2. The moon is cold. Pluto is even colder.
3. Scientists think Mercury shrank after it formed. They are not sure.
4. Venus is not the closest planet to the sun. It is the hottest.
5. Neptune has strong winds. They push clouds.
6. A space probe landed on Mars. It took photos of rocks.
7. Four planets have rings. No planet has as many rings as Saturn.
8. Does Jupiter have the most moons? Does Saturn have more?
9. Space probes circled Mars, Venus, and Mercury. They are still circling.
10. Would you like to be an astronaut? Would you prefer being a scientist?

C Tell whether each sentence contains a compound subject or a compound predicate. Write **CS** for compound subject and **CP** for compound predicate.

11. Astronauts must study and exercise.
12. Zach and I went to the planetarium.
13. We saw a sky show and heard a lecture.
14. We learned about space shuttles and asked questions.
15. Venus and Mercury are closest to the sun.
16. Plants and animals could not live on Venus.

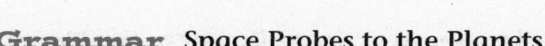

Review and Assess

Write the correct conjunction in ( ) to complete each sentence.

1. Mars is called the Red Planet, (and, or) it is visible at night.
2. Mars is the fourth planet from the sun, (or, but) it is neither big nor small.
3. Scientists are not sure if there were plants (but, and) animals on Mars.
4. Is there water on the surface of Mars, (but, or) is it dry?
5. The rocks on Earth (but, and) Mars are much alike.

Write the letter of the word that completes each sentence.

6. Astronomers are scientists who study stars _____ planets.

    A of   **C** and
    B but   **D** if

7. Carl Sagan _____ Edwin Hubble were famous astronomers.

    A and   **C** but
    B since   **D** maybe

8. The planets are far away, _____ they appear near through a telescope.

    A or   **C** but
    B and   **D** not

9. You might see Venus, _____ only when the sky is clear.

    A or   **C** and
    B but   **D** for

10. Will there be a new moon _____ a full moon?

    A but   **C** and
    B so   **D** or

Using Conjunctions to Improve Your Style

Good writing has a pleasant rhythm. Use conjunctions to combine choppy sentences and make your writing smoother.

- **Choppy:** Mercury is the first planet from the sun. Venus is the second planet. Earth is the third planet.
- **Smoother:** Mercury, Venus, and Earth are the first three planets from the sun.

A Complete each sentence below by adding a conjunction.

1. Studying meteorites is both interesting _____ educational.
2. Meteorites are bits of the solar system that have entered Earth's atmosphere, burned, _____ fallen to the ground. **3.** Scientists study meteorites to learn how old the universe is _____ what it is made of.
4. Scientists have found many small meteorites, _____ huge ones are rare. **5.** Whether large _____ small, meteorites are fascinating.

B Make the paragraph flow smoothly by combining short sentences. Finish the last sentence by adding a conjunction and more information. Write the new paragraph.

6. Space travel is exciting. It is full of adventure. **7.** Astronauts have landed on the moon. They have not visited any planets yet.
8. Some space probes have landed on planets. Others are circling in space. **9.** A planet may be sizzling hot. It may be freezing.
10. Several planets have rings. Earth is the only planet with life.
11. An astronaut's life is exciting, (but, and, or) _____.

C Write your impressions of space travel. Use conjunctions to make your sentences flow smoothly.

Writing a Summary

Some **tests** may ask you to summarize information from a time line, diagram, or chart. You will need to read the information carefully and shape it into your own sentences. Follow the tips below.

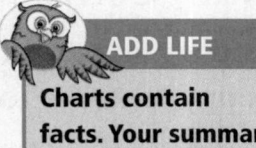

ADD LIFE

Charts contain facts. Your summary should bring these facts to life.

About the Sun	
What it does	• Supplies heat and light to Earth • Makes life possible
Energy	• Produced by nuclear fusion • Travels in waves of particles called photons
Distance from Earth	• About 93 million miles • Closest star to Earth
Movement	• Spins around center of Milky Way galaxy
Type of body	• Large star • One of more than 100 billion stars in galaxy
Made of	• Hot gases • 75% hydrogen, 25% helium

Organize your ideas. In a time line, information will already be arranged in order. With a chart or diagram, you will need to decide how to present information. In any case, you must put words into complete sentences and provide a beginning and a conclusion.

Write a good beginning. You might engage readers with a thought-provoking question.

Develop and elaborate ideas. Include all important details from the chart. Make sure the details support your main idea.

Write a strong ending. Try to write a "clincher" sentence to provide a clear ending. You might add a final comment of your own.

Check your work. Ask a classmate to read your summary. Are there places that need more details or clearer information?

See how the summary below is based on information from the chart, along with the writer's own comment and sentences.

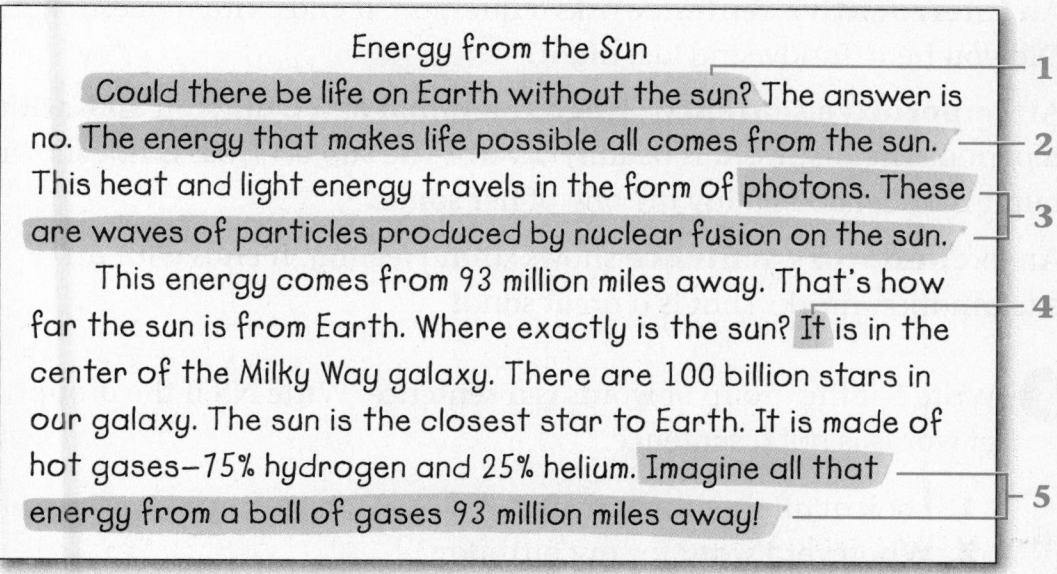

Energy from the Sun

Could there be life on Earth without the sun? The answer is — 1
no. The energy that makes life possible all comes from the sun. — 2
This heat and light energy travels in the form of photons. These — 3
are waves of particles produced by nuclear fusion on the sun.
    This energy comes from 93 million miles away. That's how — 4
far the sun is from Earth. Where exactly is the sun? It is in the
center of the Milky Way galaxy. There are 100 billion stars in
our galaxy. The sun is the closest star to Earth. It is made of
hot gases—75% hydrogen and 25% helium. Imagine all that — 5
energy from a ball of gases 93 million miles away!

1. The opening question grabs the reader's attention.
2. This sentence states the main idea.
3. The writer explains a technical term.
4. Use of the pronoun *it* avoids repeating "the sun."
5. This ending returns to the main idea—the power of energy—and reveals the writer's voice.

Sentences and Punctuation

A **sentence** is a group of words that can be a statement, a question, a command, a request, or an exclamation. It begins with a capital letter and ends with a punctuation mark. A sentence always expresses a complete thought.

A **declarative sentence** makes a statement. It ends with a period: Tandy is a talented singer.

An **interrogative sentence** asks a question. It ends with a question mark: Did you hear Tandy sing last night?

An **imperative sentence** gives a command or a request. It ends with a period. The first word is usually a verb. The subject *(you)* is not shown, but it is understood: Play me one of her songs.

An **exclamatory sentence** shows strong feeling. It ends with an exclamation mark: That is a great song!

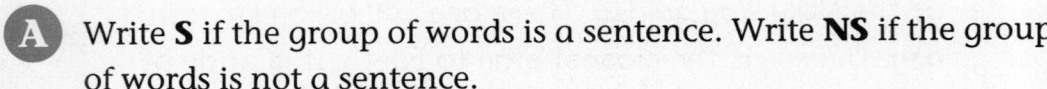 **A** Write **S** if the group of words is a sentence. Write **NS** if the group of words is not a sentence.

1. Look at all the instruments!
2. Whatever I want for my birthday?
3. That saxophone in the store window.
4. How to play the guitar?
5. What do you think about playing the drums?
6. That would really keep the neighbors up!
7. Play something for me.
8. Wow, your playing makes my ears ring!

B Read each sentence. Write **declarative, interrogative, imperative,** or **exclamatory** to identify which type of sentence it is.

1. I like to listen to music.
2. What kind of music do you like?
3. I listen to jazz at night and rock during the day.
4. I think jazz is fantastic!
5. Please hand me that CD over there.
6. Which one do you want me to give you?
7. Give me the one with the blue cover.
8. Do you mean this one?
9. Yes, that's the one I mean.
10. Wow, I've never heard such a loud song!

C Rewrite each sentence with correct capitalization and end punctuation.

11. my aunt and uncle are coming to visit us
12. what will we do during their visit
13. aunt Alice promised to teach me some new dance steps
14. wow, she can dance better than anyone I know
15. she has won many contests and has dozens of trophies
16. show me your best moves
17. can we enter the dance contest at the community center
18. it would be awesome if we won

Review and Assess

Rewrite each sentence with correct capitalization and end punctuation.

1. what a musical family I have
2. my brother Darrell is a singer
3. have you heard my mom sing
4. doesn't she have a beautiful voice
5. listen to this tape I made

Read each group of words. Write the letter of the answer that describes those words.

6. What a catchy tune that is!

    A declarative sentence   **C** imperative sentence
    B exclamatory sentence   **D** not a sentence

7. I've never heard that one before.

    A declarative sentence   **C** imperative sentence
    B interrogative sentence   **D** exclamatory sentence

8. Is it new?

    A declarative sentence   **C** imperative sentence
    B interrogative sentence   **D** not a sentence

9. Some hip-hop on the radio.

    A declarative sentence   **C** imperative sentence
    B interrogative sentence   **D** not a sentence

10. Turn it up, please.

    A declarative sentence   **C** imperative sentence
    B interrogative sentence   **D** exclamatory sentence

Varying Sentences in Your Writing

Use different kinds of sentences to make your writing persuasive.

- Have you listened to Miles Davis's *Kind of Blue?* It's one of the most important albums in the history of jazz. Get a copy and listen to it.

A Choose the best sentence from the box to complete the paragraph below. Then add end punctuation and write the new paragraph.

> Maybe the dance will be more fun if we try harder.
> Everyone had better agree with me.
> If everyone dances, this will be a great party!
> Can we all bring some old CDs to exchange?

1. I think we should play different kinds of music at the school dance__ **2.** Why should we limit the types of songs the DJ will play__ **3.** Do we have to play one kind of music__ **4.** Different kinds of music will make everybody dance __ **5.** _____

B Persuade a friend to go to a concert with you and your family. Add an interrogative sentence and an imperative sentence. Then write the new paragraph.

> The Streaking Airplane is our favorite band. Just wait till you hear them. The band is terrific! Be sure to bring earplugs, though. They play fast and loud.

C Write a persuasive argument to your principal. Try to persuade him or her to invite your favorite band or musician to play at your school. Use different kinds of sentences.

Capitalization

Use a **capital letter** to begin a **sentence.**

- **T**he colorful pottery is made out of clay.

Capitalize the first word and every important word of a **proper noun.** Proper nouns name particular persons, places, or things.

- The pottery from **N**ew **M**exico is especially beautiful.

Capitalize the first letter of an **abbreviation.** Many abbreviations end in a period. Capitalize both letters in an abbreviation of a state name for a mailing address, but do not use a period.

- 1923 Olivera **S**t.
  Santa Fe, **NM**

Capitalize days of the week and months of the year.

- The store is open on **S**aturdays in **M**ay.

Also capitalize **titles** before people's names.

- The owner of the pottery store is **M**r. Harris.

 A Rewrite each sentence using correct capitalization.

1. my neighbor, mrs. smith, is a talented folk artist.
2. her mailing address is 45 flores st., tempe, az.
3. she is a navajo, and she weaves rugs.
4. many navajo live in colorado.
5. colorado and arizona share a border.
6. the southwest museum of art has rugs and pottery.
7. the museum is open evenings in june and july.
8. admission is free on thursdays.

B Write **C** if the group of words is capitalized correctly. If the group of words is capitalized incorrectly, rewrite it using correct capitalization.

1. Tucson, Az
2. 2563 blue jay avenue
3. mr. Harold greene
4. El Paso University
5. san Antonio spurs
6. rocky mountains
7. Butte, MT
8. 624 ford street
9. my best friend jerry
10. dr. valenzuela

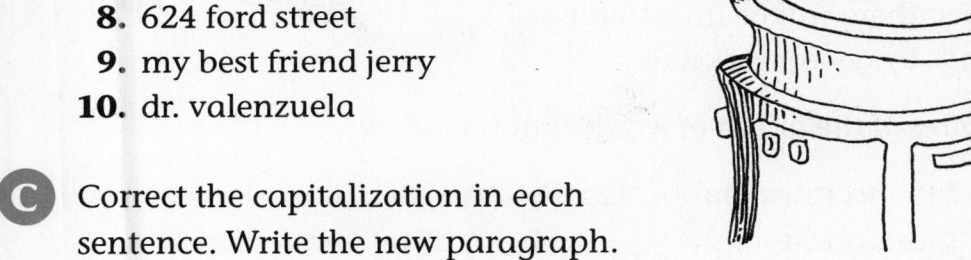

C Correct the capitalization in each sentence. Write the new paragraph.

11. Last saturday, Maria went to a pottery-making group. 12. it was her first time at the Mesa verde School for the Arts. 13. The class will meet during june and july. 14. Her teacher, glenda Robbins, knows a lot about making pottery. 15. She began the class by showing the students pictures of pottery made by the navajo. 16. maria took a ball of clay and rolled it between her fingers. 17. She made a tall jar like the one she had seen in the clayworld crafts Shop. 18. When maria was done, she put her pot in the kiln to bake. 19. Mrs. robbins said she could pick it up next thursday.

Review and Assess

Rewrite each sentence using correct capitalization.

1. Vera's family lives in taos, new mexico.
2. they like to do crafts together.
3. Vera's sister, elois, makes bowls out of wood.
4. her father, mr. Briggs, teaches pottery.
5. He teaches at sonoma state university.
6. On saturdays the family goes to craft fairs.
7. They also visit the taos art museum.
8. In august there will be an exhibit of paintings by georgia o'keeffe.

Write the letter of the group of words that is correct.

9. **A** Taos art museum
   B Taos art Museum
   C Taos Art Museum
   D Taos Art museum

10. **A** Phoenix, az
    B phoenix, az
    C phoenix, Az
    D Phoenix, AZ

11. **A** saturday, may 12
    B Saturday, May 12
    C saturday, May 12
    D Saturday, MAY 12

12. **A** my sister, Juana lopez
    B my sister, Juana Lopez
    C My Sister, juana Lopez
    D my sister, juana lopez

13. **A** Dr. david denny
    B DR. david Denny
    C Dr. David Denny
    D dr. David Denny

14. **A** Dear Ms. Levine:
    B Dear ms. Levine:
    C Dear MS Levine:
    D dear ms. Levine:

Observing the Rules for Capitalization

A well-written persuasive argument flows smoothly. It avoids mistakes with capital letters that would confuse the reader.

A Match the number of each sentence in the paragraph with the correction that it needs.

    A Capitalize the first word of a sentence.
    B Capitalize proper nouns that name people.
    C Capitalize names of months.
    D Capitalize both letters of state name abbreviations.
    E Capitalize proper nouns that name places.

    1. You'll love the art show at the chapman museum. **2.** Many friends are showing works, including john rico and Jenny Toomey. **3.** the colorful paintings and crafts are terrific! **4.** Order a catalogue for the show by sending two dollars to 123 N. Oak Avenue, Salt Lake City, ut. **5.** Don't miss this show, which runs through may 8.

B Correct errors in capitalization in this paragraph. Then write your own opening and closing sentences to persuade people to visit the show. You might write about who would enjoy the show and where it is located. Write the new paragraph.

    6. _____ **7.** sunday I went to a show at the Museum of art in fontville. **8.** the show includes fascinating works by artists such as Tony charo. **9.** The show ends july 8. **10.** _____

C Write a note persuading a friend to join you at a real or an imaginary art show. Use facts and opinions in your note. Be sure to use correct capitalization.

Commas

- **Commas** are used to separate items in a *series*.

  Langston traveled to Mexico, Russia, and France.

- Commas are used to speak to, or address, a person by name. This is called **direct address.** Use commas when the name is at the beginning, in the middle, or at the end of a sentence.

  Terry, have you ever read the poems of Langston Hughes?
  Yes, Eric, I have.   I wrote this poem, Terry.

- Commas follow *introductory words* in sentences.

  No, I haven't read any poems by Robert Frost.
  Wow, she's smart!

- Commas are used in *dates* and *addresses*:

  Between the day and the month: Saturday, June 23
  Between the date and the year: I started school on September 7, 2002.
  Between the city and the state: We lived in Canton, Ohio, in 2003.
  After the street address, the city, and the ZIP code, if the address
      appears in the middle of a sentence: My friend Taylor lived at 42
      N. Foster Ave., Johnstown, Pennsylvania 19876, until last year.

 Write the sentences. Add commas as needed to each sentence.

1. Langston Hughes was born in Joplin Missouri, on February 1 1902.
2. He grew up in Lawrence Kansas.
3. His grandmother told him stories about her husband uncles and herself.
4. Barb do you like the poetry of Langston Hughes?
5. Yes I like reading his poetry.

B Read each sentence. Write **C** if commas are used correctly. If commas are not used correctly, rewrite the sentence adding commas as needed.

1. Langston Hughes had an early interest in books opera and plays.
2. My uncle has taken us to concerts, plays, and poetry readings.
3. Truly he loves all the arts.
4. Uncle Serge wrote his first poem on April 14 1967.
5. That day he was sad tired, and lonely.
6. Yes he wrote about those feelings in that first poem.
7. Now Uncle Serge writes poetry, composes music, and draws pictures.
8. Wow Uncle Serge has been writing for almost 40 years!
9. Do you think I could be a great writer Uncle Serge?
10. Perhaps I could dance, sing, or sculpt instead.

C Write sentences that tell a day of the week and a date you could do each activity. Add commas as needed. The first one is done for you.

11. riding a bike <u>I will ride my bike on Friday, March 30.</u>
12. writing a short story
13. taking a train trip
14. visiting relatives
15. going to the zoo
16. going to a movie
17. sleeping late

Opens Friday, May 1

Review and Assess

Rewrite the sentences adding commas as needed.

1. Langston Hughes Rita Dove and Robert Frost are fine poets.
2. Angela have you read anything by these writers?
3. Yes Heidi I read a book of Rita Dove's poems.
4. It's from the library at 321 Hill Street Bend Oregon.
5. Finally I know where I can find that book.

Write the letter of the phrase that uses commas correctly to complete each sentence.

6. Susanne dreamed of becoming an astronaut, _____.

   A a doctor or a lawyer.   **C** a doctor or, a lawyer
   B a, doctor, or a lawyer   **D** a doctor, or a lawyer

7. Eric dreamed of moving to _____.

   A Brooklyn New York,   **C** Brooklyn, New York
   B Brooklyn, New, York   **D** Brooklyn New York

8. Can you _____ have ever met a famous artist?

   A tell me, Dad, if you   **C** tell me Dad if you
   B tell, me Dad if you   **D** tell me Dad if you,

9. My father was born on _____.

   A April 17, 1961   **C** April 17 1961
   B April, 17, 1961   **D** April, 17 1961

10. We have lived in _____ since 1996.

    A Dubuque, Iowa.   **C** Dubuque, Iowa,
    B Dubuque Iowa   **D** Dubuque Iowa,

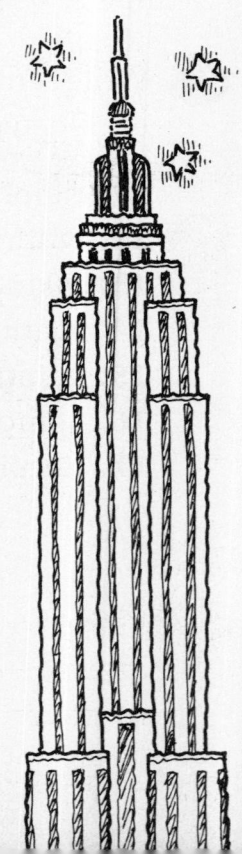

Making Writing Clear with Commas

Commas make your writing easier to read. They can also strengthen your persuasive argument. Set off introductory words and phrases, such as *clearly* and *best of all,* with commas to mark your strongest statements.

A Match each sentence with the letter of the rule it should follow. Write the sentences correctly.

  A Use commas to separate items in a series.
  B Use commas with direct address.
  C Use commas after introductory phrases.
  D Use commas to separate the day and the month.
  E Use commas between the date and the year.

1. Saturday March 16, is the date of our book fair. **2.** The fair on March 8 2003, was a rousing success. **3.** The fair will raise money for field trips supplies and books. **4.** Parents you should take your children. **5.** Best of all the fair is free for kids under twelve.

B Add commas as needed to the sentences below. Write a closing sentence of your own. Write the new paragraph.

6. Anyone who wants to become an interesting poet playwright or novelist should travel. **7.** Travel teaches you about new people places and things. **8.** I went to Ghana on April 7 2003. **9.** I learned about Ghana's people customs and language. **10.** Clearly my trip to Ghana has made me a more informed writer. **11.** _____

C Write a persuasive argument to convince your teacher to have the class read your favorite book. Be sure to use commas correctly to set off information.

Quotations and Quotation Marks

A speaker's exact words are called a **quotation.** When you write a quotation, use **quotation marks ("/")** at the beginning and end of the speaker's exact words.

- Begin the quotation with a capital letter: He replied, "We knew that."
- If the quotation comes last in a sentence, use a comma to separate it from the rest of the sentence: Ben Franklin said, "A penny saved is a penny earned."
- If the quotation comes first, use a comma, a question mark, or an exclamation mark to separate the quotation from the rest of the sentence: "She's a genius!" he claimed.
- Periods and commas at the end of quotations come before the quotation mark: "Don't be too sure," she warned.
- If the quotation is a question or an exclamation, put the question mark or exclamation mark before the end quotation mark: "What a great invention!" he shouted.

A Write the sentence in each pair that uses quotation marks correctly.

1. "Have you ever been to Philadelphia?" asked Justin.
   "Have you ever been to Philadelphia? asked Justin."
2. "My cousin and I grew up there", I answered.
   "My cousin and I grew up there," I answered.
3. "I added, What a great city!"
   I added, "What a great city!"
4. Did you know that Franklin lived in Europe? "Sal asked."
   "Did you know that Franklin lived in Europe?" Sal asked.

B Add quotation marks and rewrite each sentence.

1. What do you think was the most important invention ever? asked Lou.
2. That's an interesting question, said James.
3. He added, I think electricity was a very important invention.
4. Without electricity there would be no television, agreed Lou.
5. That would be terrible! Lou added.
6. James asked, Can you imagine what life would be like without TV?
7. No, I can't, said Lou.
8. I think it might have been fun to live without TV, James suggested.
9. Lou asked, You're joking, aren't you?
10. James thought and said, We'd have more time to talk to each other.

C Rewrite each sentence. Add quotation marks and other correct punctuation as needed.

11. My teacher asked me What do you want to be when you grow up
12. I answered I guess I'd like to be an inventor
13. You need a lot of patience said my teacher
14. Would you like to borrow some books about inventors she asked
15. That would be great I said
16. Could you find me a book about Elijah McCoy I asked
17. My teacher responded I have one that I think you'll enjoy

Review and Assess

Add quotation marks and rewrite each sentence.

1. What are you learning about science in school? asked my father.
2. I learned about Dian Fossey, I answered.
3. She did some amazing research! Dad said.
4. He added, She studied gorillas in their natural habitat.
5. That's really impressive! I replied.

Write the letter of the answer that completes each sentence correctly.

6. "Yesterday I read about Benjamin Franklin and his _____ said Romi.

   A almanac   **C** almanac,"
   B almanac"   **D** almanac,

7. "Almanacs are very _____ she observed.

   A useful,"   **C** useful"
   B useful?   **D** useful

8. "Why, what's in _____ asked Darla.

   A them?   **C** them!
   B them"?   **D** them?"

9. Romi answered, _____ full of useful information."

   A "they're   **C** "They're
   B They're   **D** They're"

10. "That's great to _____ Darla said.

   A know"   **C** know
   B "Know   **D** know!"

Using Quotations to Support Your Opinions

You can support your persuasive arguments with quotations.
Use sources such as books, articles, or interviews with experts.

A Add two sentences from the box that best support the paragraph below.
Write the sentences with quotation marks and punctuation.

> My mom asked, will you sing a song for me
> Ms. Primeau, our band conductor, said being in the band
> teaches discipline and promotes self-confidence.
> I love that Picasso painting, Richie shouted
> Mr. Rossetti, our art teacher, said in an interview learning
> about color and design is a valuable life skill.

Cutting art and music would be a bad move. These classes help
us learn other skills. We improve math skills when we measure out
precise quantities of blue and yellow paint to make a certain shade
of green. We learn history when we study a composer's life. The most
important arguments come from two experts.

B Add quotation marks and punctuation to each sentence.
Then add a final sentence with a quotation of your own.

1. John said a shelter would provide a safe place for stray animals.
2. These animals can't survive outside added our vet. **3.** I'll bet we could
get student volunteers to help offered Principal O'Leary **4.** I said _____.

C Write an argument to persuade your principal to name your school
after a famous person. Use quotations to support your argument.

Review of Compound and Complex Sentences

A **compound sentence** contains two simple sentences. They are joined by a comma and a conjunction such as *and, but,* or *or.* The two sentences must have ideas that go together.

A **complex sentence** is made by combining a simple sentence with a group of words that cannot stand on its own as a sentence. This group of words has a subject and a predicate and often begins with a word such as *because, if, as,* or *when.* When this group of words begins a sentence, it is usually followed by a comma.

- **Simple sentences:** Our bird was lost. I could not find her.
- **Compound sentence:** Our bird was lost, and I could not find her.
- **Complex sentence:** When I examined the cage, I noticed the latch was broken.

A Read the paragraph. Write **compound** or **complex** to identify each sentence.

1. Andrea's pet lizard had slithered out of his tank, and he was nowhere to be found. **2.** She didn't know what to do, and she felt just awful. **3.** When her brother got home, he offered to help Andrea look. **4.** They searched every corner of the room, but the lizard had disappeared into thin air. **5.** Andrea refused to give up the search because she really loved Lizard Louie. **6.** The kids searched their rooms, and they searched the kitchen. **7.** Louie could be in a closet, or maybe he slid down a drain. **8.** As they were about to give up, they saw something scoot by. **9.** Andrea scooped up her lizard, and they had a happy reunion.

B You can make a sentence by matching a group of words in column one with a group of words in column two. Match the number with the letter.

1. I begged for a dog
2. After I do homework,
3. When she gets hot,
4. If I eat a cookie,
5. She likes cats,
6. She chases squirrels,
7. Her fur is brown,
8. She usually smells nice,
9. She is my best friend
10. If you get a pet,

A. we run to the park.
B. or she runs after balls.
C. until I got Taffy.
D. she begs for crumbs.
E. but she stinks sometimes.
F. she pants.
G. I'd suggest a dog.
H. but she hates mice.
I. and so are her eyes.
J. because she's fun and loyal.

C Add a simple sentence to each sentence part to form a compound or a complex sentence. Write the new sentences with correct punctuation.

11. When my class went on a field trip _____
12. Because we were studying animal behavior _____
13. As the dolphins leaped _____
14. _____ and the trainer rewarded them
15. _____ but I liked the dolphins best

Review and Assess

Write **compound** or **complex** to identify the kind of sentence.

1. Duane holds his pet parrot, and he strokes its feathers.
2. When the big bird is hungry, it shrieks loudly.
3. Because the parrot loves Duane, it sits on his shoulder.
4. Duane loves this silly bird, but he hates cleaning its cage.
5. At night, the bird plays with Duane, or it takes a nap.

Write the letter of the word you would use to complete each sentence of the paragraph.

   6. Owning a pet is a big responsibility, _____ you have to be willing to work hard. **7.** _____ it is such a big responsibility, not everyone should own a pet. **8.** You need to feed your pet every day, _____ you should do your best to keep it clean. **9.** It can be difficult taking care of a pet, _____ it is well worth the effort. **10.** _____ you are sad, most pets know it and will make you feel better.

6.   **A** but   **C** when
     B and   **D** or

7.   **A** And   **C** Because
     B But   **D** Or

8.   **A** when   **G** because
     B and   **D** or

9.   **A** or   **C** when
     B because   **D** but

10. **A** When   **C** But
     B And   **D** Or

Varying Sentences to Strengthen Your Style

Use compound and complex sentences to enrich your writing style.
Combine short, choppy sentences to make your writing livelier.

- I think we should have a class pet. Pets are educational.
  Our class could observe the pet. We could write a class report.
- I think we should have a class pet because pets are educational.
  Our class could observe the pet, and we could write a class report.

A Combine each pair of sentences below using the word in ( ).
Add a comma if necessary. Write the paragraph.

1. I don't think students should bring their pets to school. Pets
can be distracting. (because) **2.** Everyone loves animals. Animals
need a lot of attention. (but) **3.** Students must concentrate on their
work. They should pay attention to their teachers. (and) **4.** However,
we could have a class pet. Students pledge to help care for it. (if)
5. The teacher must set firm rules for caring for a class pet.
Students must follow them. (and)

B Complete the sentences below by making them compound or
complex. Write the new sentences.

6. I believe zoo animals should not be kept in cages because
_____. **7.** When they are allowed to roam freely _____. **8.** _____
because they would get more exercise and stay healthier in the
wild. **9.** These animals are amazing to watch, but _____.
10. When I visit the zoo next time _____.

C Write a letter to your school paper persuading students to be zoo
volunteers. Use compound and complex sentences.

Writing a Persuasive Argument

A **test** may ask you to write a persuasive argument. Support your opinion with reasons and use words such as *should* and *best*. Follow the tips below.

CHECK FACTS

Support your persuasive argument with facts from reliable sources.

Understand the prompt. Make sure you know what to do. Read the prompt carefully. A prompt for a persuasive argument could look like this:

> **"Chocolate Is Missing" is the first chapter of *The Great Ideas of Lila Fenwick*. Write an argument persuading your classmates to select that book or another book you like to be the next read-aloud. Support your opinion with reasons.**

Key words are *argument, persuading, support,* and *opinion.*

Find a good topic. Think of books your classmates might enjoy. Narrow your list by asking yourself: *What arguments could I use to persuade my classmates to read this book?*

Organize your ideas. Write an opinion chart on scratch paper. State your opinion and list reasons that support it.

STATEMENT OF OPINION	REASONS
I think we should read <u>Pinocchio</u> for the next class read-aloud.	• Famous story • Interesting characters and plot • About a puppet who wants to be a boy • Exciting to hear the words read • Pinocchio has dreams.

Write a good beginning. Write a strong topic sentence that expresses your opinion. Let readers know how you feel right away.

Develop and elaborate ideas. Use your chart to review details that support your opinion. Decide which reason is most important. Use persuasive words to make your argument stronger.

Write a strong ending. Write a powerful ending to "wrap up" your argument.

Check your work. Reread your writing and make any necessary changes.

See how the persuasive argument below addresses the prompt, has a strong beginning, and stays focused on the topic.

Read Along with Me

1 — Some books are just meant to be read aloud. I think Pinocchio would be a great read-aloud book for our class.

2 — Pinocchio is a famous tale read by kids all over the world. The interesting characters and plot make you want to keep reading. Hearing the story read aloud makes it more exciting. I think the idea of a puppet coming to life is really neat. After we read the story, we should watch the movie.

3 — The best reason to read Pinocchio is that the main character is just like us. Everybody has dreams, and we want — 4 to see them come true. Our class should read this book to — 5 learn its message— follow your dreams and don't give up!

1. The first sentence makes the reader want to know more.
2. The writer uses persuasive words effectively.
3. Argument builds to the most important reason.
4. A compound sentence makes the writing flow smoothly.
5. This strong ending sums up the writer's thoughts.

INDEX

A

Abbreviations, 138–141
Action verbs. *See* Verbs.
Addresses. *See* Commas.
Adjectives, 90–93
  articles, 90–93
  comparative, 98–101, 111
  in sentences, 94–97
  in writing, 93, 97, 101
  superlative, 98–101
Adverbs, 102–105
  in sentences, 106–109
  in writing, 105, 109
Agreement
  pronoun, 120–123
  verb, 72–74, 84–87
Antecedents. *See* Referents.
Apostrophe
  in contractions, 116–119
  in possessive nouns, 62–65
Articles, 90–93
Assess, 26, 30, 34, 38, 42, 48, 52, 56,
  60, 64, 70, 74, 78, 82, 86, 92, 96, 100,
  104, 108, 114, 118, 122, 126, 130,
  136, 140, 144, 148, 152

B

Be. *See* Verbs.

C

Capitalization
  abbreviations, 138–141
  days of the week, 50–53, 138–141
  first word of sentence, 24–31,
    138–141
  I, 112
  in writing, 138–141
  months of the year, 138–141
  names of people, 50–53
  names of places, 50–53
  states, 50–53, 138–141
  titles of people, 138–141
Charts, 14, 88, 110, 132, 154
Commands. *See* Sentences.
Commas
  addresses, 142–145
  dates, 142–145
  direct address, 142–145
  in compound sentences, 40–43,
    150–153
  in quotations, 146–149
  introductory words, 142–145
  in writing, 145
  series, 142–145
Common nouns. *See* Nouns.
Comparative adjectives, 98–101
Comparison/contrast writing. *See*
  Writing, types of.

Comparisons
   simile, 75
   with adjectives, 101
Complex sentences. *See* Sentences.
Compound predicate. *See* Predicates.
Compound sentences. *See* Sentences.
Compound subject. *See* Subjects.
Conjunctions, 128–131, 150–153
Contractions, 116–119
Conventions. *See* Writing.

D

Dates. *See* Commas.
Declarative sentences. *See* Sentences.
Describing words. *See* Adjectives.
Descriptive writing. *See* Writing.
Details, 6, 31, 94, 97, 106–109, 127, 133
Direct address. *See* Commas.
Directions. *See* Writing, How-to report.

E

Elaboration, 45, 67, 89, 111, 133, 155
End marks. *See* Sentences.
Exclamation mark, 36–39, 134–137
Exclamations. *See* Sentences.
Exclamatory sentences. *See* Sentences.

F

Facts to support opinion, 154–155

H

Helping verbs. *See* Verbs.
How-to writing. *See* Writing.

I

I, 112
Ideas and content. *See* Writing.
Imperative sentences. *See* Sentences.
Improving sentences, 94–97, 106–109
Interrogative sentences. *See* Sentences.
Introductory words. *See* Commas.
Irregular verbs. *See* Verbs.

J

Joining words. *See* Conjunctions.

L

Linking verbs. *See* Verbs.

M

Main idea, 6–7, 133
Main verb. *See* Verbs.
Mechanics
   apostrophe, 62–65, 116–118
   comma, 40–43, 142–145, 146–149, 150–153
   exclamation mark, 36–39, 134–137
   period, 24–27, 32–35, 36–39, 134–137
   question mark, 32–35, 134–137

N

Narrative writing. *See* Writing.
Narrowing a topic, 6
Notes, 44
Nouns
   common, 46–49
   exact, 49
   in writing, 49, 57, 61
   irregular, 58–61
   names of days and months, 50–53,
      138–141
   names of people, 50–53, 138–141
   names of places, 50–53, 138–141
   plural, 54–57, 58–61
   possessive, 62–65
   proper, 50–53, 138–141
      in writing, 53
   regular, 54–57
   singular, 54–57
   states, 50–53, 138–141
   titles of people, 138–141

O

Object of preposition, 124–127
Object pronouns. *See* Pronouns.
Opinion, 149, 154–155
Order words, 44, 105, 111
Organization. *See* Writing.

P

Period, 24–27, 36–39, 134–135
Personal narrative. *See* Writing.
Persuasive writing. *See* Writing.
Phrases, 112, 124–127
Plural nouns. *See* Nouns.
Possessive nouns. *See* Nouns.
Predicates
   complete, 28–31
   compound, 128–131
   simple, 28–31
Prepositional phrases, 124–127
Prepositions, 124–127
Prompts, 19, 44, 66, 88, 110, 154
Pronouns
   in contractions, 116–119
   in writing, 115, 119, 123
   object, 116–119
   possessive, 112–115
   referents, 120–123
   subject, 116–119
Proofreading, 16–17
Proper nouns. *See* Nouns.
Punctuation, 24–27, 32–35, 36–39,
   134–135. *See also* Mechanics.
Purpose for writing, 6–7

Q

Question mark, 32–35, 134–135
Questions. *See* Sentences.
Quotations, 146–149
   in writing, 149
Quotation marks, 146–149

R

Reasons to support opinions, 154–155

Referents, 120–123

Research report. *See* Writing.

Review, 26, 30, 34, 38, 42, 48, 52, 56, 60, 64, 70, 74, 78, 82, 86, 92, 96, 100, 104, 108, 114, 118, 122, 126, 130, 136, 140, 144, 148, 152

Rubrics, 18

S

Sentence combining, 43, 153

Sentences
  capitalization in, 24–27, 138–141
  complex, 14–15, 40–43, 150–153
  compound, 14–15, 40–43, 128–131, 150–153
  declarative, 14–15, 32–35, 134–137
  exclamatory, 14–15, 36–39, 134–137
  imperative, 14–15, 36–39, 134–137
  interrogative, 14–15, 32–35, 134–137
  punctuation of, 24–27, 32–35, 36–39, 134–137
  simple, 40, 150–153

Series. *See* Commas.

Simile, 75

Singular nouns. *See* Nouns.

Statements. *See* Sentences.

Strategies. *See* Writing.

Style, 35, 39, 43, 65, 71, 83, 87, 131, 137, 153

Subjects, 28–31
  complete, 28–31
  compound, 128–131
  simple, 28–31

Subject pronouns. *See* Pronouns.

Summary, 132–133

Superlative adjectives, 98–101

T

Tenses, 76–79, 80–83, 84–87

Tests. *See* Writing for tests.

Time-order words. *See* Order words.

Titles
  of people, 138–141

Topics, 6–7, 44, 66, 88, 110, 132, 154

Traits of good writing, 6–7, 8–9, 10–11, 12–13, 14–15, 16–17, 18–22

V

Venn diagram, 8

Verbs
  action, 68–71, 84–87
  agreement, 72–75, 84–87
  be, 68–71, 72–75, 84–87
  future tense, 76–79, 84–87
  helping, 68–71, 84–87
  in comparisons, 75
  in sentences, 72–75
  irregular, 80–83, 84–87
  is, am, are, was, were, 68–71, 72–75, 84–87

linking, 68–71, 84–87
main, 68–71
past tense, 76–79, 80–83
present tense, 76–79, 80–83
Vivid words, 12–13, 75
Voice. *See* Writing.

W
Web, 66
Word choice. *See* Writing.
Writing
conventions, 16–17, 18–22
details, 6, 31, 94, 97, 106–109,
    127, 133
ideas and content, 6–7, 18–22,
    44–45, 66–67, 88–89, 110–111,
    132–133, 154–155
main idea, 6–7
models, 19–22, 45, 67, 89, 111, 133,
    155
organization, 8–9, 18–22, 44, 66, 88,
    105, 110, 132, 154

prompts, 19, 44, 66, 88, 110, 154
strategies, 6, 8, 10, 12, 14, 16
types of
    comparison/contrast essay, 71,
        75, 79, 83, 87, 88–89
    description, 49, 53, 57, 61, 65,
        66–67
    how–to report, 93, 97, 101, 105,
        109, 110–111
    personal narrative, 27, 31, 35, 39,
        43, 44–45
    persuasive argument, 137, 141,
        145, 149, 153, 154–155
    research report, 115, 119, 123,
        127, 131
    summary, 132–133
voice, 10–11, 18–22, 39
word choice, 12–13, 18–22, 49, 53,
    71, 79, 83, 87, 93, 97, 109
Writing for tests, 44–45, 66–67,
    88–89, 110–111, 132–133, 154–155

Art Acknowledgments
Franklin Hammond 7, 8, 10, 21, 37, 48, 70, 78, 100, 113, 118, 143, 147
Rose Mary Berlin 13, 17, 22, 41, 42, 47, 55, 56, 59, 60, 64, 85, 107, 122, 129, 140,
148 Yvette Santiago Banek 25, 29, 33, 51, 63, 69, 73, 77, 81, 82, 95, 103, 116,
139, 144, 152